VITAL POINTS IN DEMONSTRATION

YOU CAN GET WHAT YOU WANT IF YOU RETURN HOME

DR. ROBERT A. RUSSELL

Audio Enlightenment Press

Giving Voice to the Wisdom of the Ages

Printed in the United States of America

First Printing, 2022
ISBN 978-1-941489-93-2

www.RobertARussell.Org

Note To The Student

This book is one of a series of three consecutive metaphysical studies on the Parable of the Prodigal Son and the Elder Brother. The books are listed in the order that they should be read.

1. YOU CAN GET WHAT YOU WANT IF YOU FIND IT WITHIN YOURSELF.

2. VITAL POINTS IN DEMONSTRATION.
   You Can Get What You Want
   If You Return Home.

3. THE QUICKEST WAY TO EVERYTHING GOOD.
   You Can Get What You Want
   If You Put This First.

4. CHANGE YOUR THOUGHT AND TAKE IT.
   You Can Get What You Want
   If You Change Your Consciousness.

Table of Contents

LIFE AS IT IS, AND AS PLANNED BY GOD . . .

HEALTH, SUCCESS, JOY, HAPPINESS, STRENGTH, DOMINION, WEALTH, FAITH, CONFIDENCE, CERTAINTY, PEACE, POWER, PLENTY, POISE, COURAGE, LOVE, HARMONY, FREEDOM

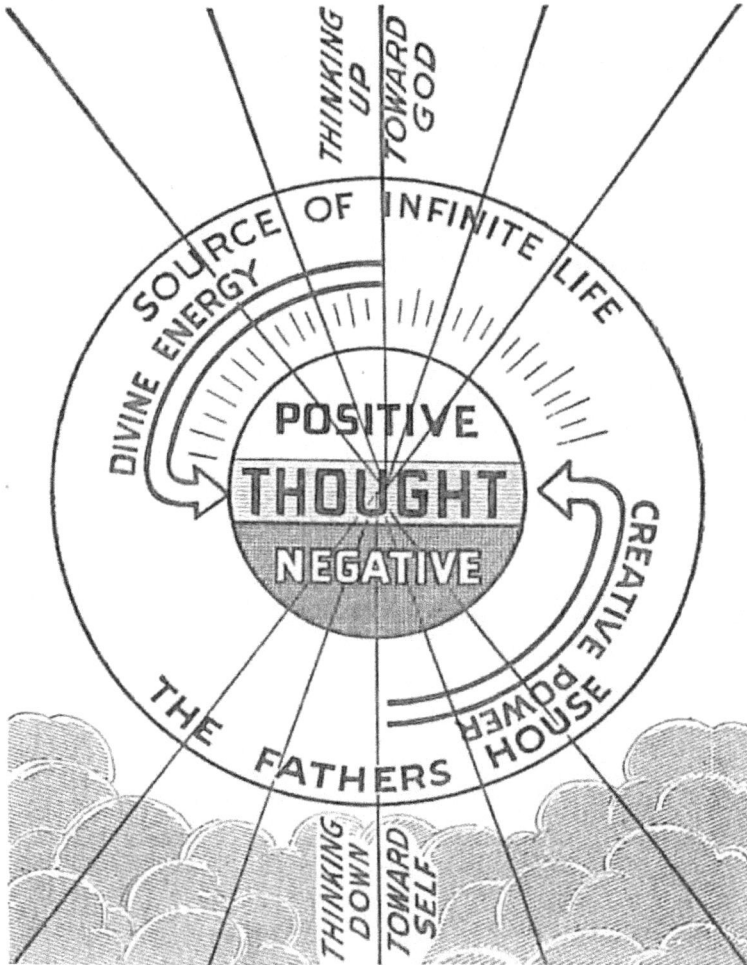

DISEASE, FAILURE, SORROW, MISERY, WEAKNESS, INFERIORITY, POVERTY, UNHAPPINESS, WORRY, FEAR, DOUBT, LOSS, TROUBLE, LIMITATIONS, DISCORD, PROBLEMS, BONDAGE

LIFE AS WE MAKE IT BY OUR NEGATIVE THINKING

Explanation Of Diagram

If you will study the diagram on the opposite page, you will see that the power flowing God through man is neither good nor bad as the human mind usually understands it. It is simply Divine Energy — Creative Power. The energy that is turned into failure, sickness and discord and other negative expressions in no way differs from the energy that manifests in success, health, peace and other forms of good. The difference is not in the energy or Creative Power, but in the thought that turns it either into constructive channels or destructive channels.

How important it is, then, that we should keep our thought centered in the constructive and affirmative side of Good and guarded against the destructive side of evil, so that only the good can manifest in our lives — the riches of life instead of its limitations.

NOTE TO THE STUDENT

The Author asks that before beginning the study of this book you read thoughtfully the Parable of The Prodigal Son as found in the fifteenth chapter of St. Luke's Gospel.

Foreword

The ancients likened the Universe to a great mirror that gives back to man the exact reflection of his own thoughts. So it is hoped that this book and its companion volumes may serve as looking glasses in which you may see yourself as you are, to the end that you may realize the Bigger man you are capable of becoming.

These books are practical guides not only to those who have not found the way but to those who already are on the way. What you want to know is how you can get out of difficulty when you are in it, and how you can stay out. of difficulty — and how you can he successful, happy and free.

Just as there are some automobiles which hold the road better than others so there are some books that hold the road better than others. What we need is a system that will enable us to do the things which we have so long heard about and read about. We need not only to see all the machinery and how it works, but we must see it at work in ourselves.

When we get the right relationship to the Universe (establish a reciprocal action between ourselves and God), then we can steer right. And, after all, successful and balanced living is largely a matter of steering. If we steer right then the automobile will go in the right place. If we steer wrong then it will go in the wrong places.

What has been left out of this book is just as important as that which has been put in, but the author leaves this to the imagination of the reader.

R. A. R

Introduction

Just as a magnet will attract only those things which are like itself, so a man's mind will attract only those things which are like his thoughts. A magnet has no affinity for leather, clay, plastic, copper, rubber or wood, and neither has a depressed or negative state of mind an affinity for success, power, health or wealth. Just as the happy man is happy because of a specific mental attitude toward life, so the miserable man is unhappy for the same reason.

Because life is a state of consciousness, we constantly are attracting and establishing relations with persons, places, conditions and things which respond exactly to our thoughts and states of mind.

The environment in which we find ourselves, the people with whom we are associated, the particular difficulties, problems and ailments from which we suffer, all are the result of our mental affinities and the law of attraction operating through them. They have come to us because of specific mental attitudes and affinities and will remain with us until the attitude or affinity has been changed.

The great difficulty with most sick, unhappy and unsuccessful people is that they have separated themselves in some way from the great Creative Mind. They are going away from their good instead of toward it. They are not thinking with God and so are attracting the wrong things. The great rule for getting what you want is to think with God's Mind instead of with your own; to think toward God and to think with God. If you would make yourself a magnet for the good things of

1

life, then you must think with God. You must change your thought from the unwanted to the wanted condition, and then think the ideal condition with all the clarity, determination, persistency and energy that you can summon up.

It makes no difference how discouraging your present circumstances appears, how apparently unobtainable your goal, how hopeless your condition—how impossible of attainment your desires seem, if you will hold the ideal condition you wish to attain to allow any doubt to lodge in your mind, then you will rise out of your difficulties and demonstrate what you want. This is the way to attract the desirable things of life.

But the moment you begin to be anxious, to wonder, to question, to fear, to worry, to doubt, you scatter your forces and the good you are seeking is shut off. You are driving your good away by your mental attitude. You are separating yourself from it by your divided thought.

Elbert Hubbard once said: "A thought is mental dynamite. If I supply you a thought, you may remember to use it or not, but if I can make you think a thought for yourself, I have put you in a position to blast your way to freedom, power and wealth." That is what this book is for—to help you to think out and work out your own salvation, and to bring out those greater possibilities which were promised in Christ's Name.

"Experience teaches us that if we persistently drink impure water we will have physical distress as a result. Because we are not so well informed as to the effects of thought, we imagine that we can go on year after year entertaining evil and destructive thoughts without anyone knowing it and without experiencing unhappy and disastrous results. This is an error. Your thoughts not only affect your character, your conduct, your destiny, but they leave their marks upon your face and your entire physical being."

Luther Burbank goes a step farther: "As you hold loving thoughts toward every person and animal and even toward plants, stars, oceans, rivers and hills, and as you are helpful and of service to the world, so you will find yourself growing more happy each day, and with the happiness comes health and everything you want," for "we are all, through the power of our thought, masters of our fate."

In truth there is nothing you cannot get from life, nothing you cannot do, no condition you cannot overcome, no mistake you cannot correct, and no situation you cannot meet, if you will only bring your thoughts up to the Power of God and keep them there. All your needs can be met, all your adversities transmuted, all your morbid ideas sublimated, all your hurts healed, just by the simple act of keeping your thoughts up to God and by keeping your mind on the things you want.

The thing you are seeking is seeking you. It is within you awaiting your release. It is not in luck, chance, circumstances, conditions, influence, persons, places and things; it is in you. Deep in the submerged depths of your being is the Power that will, when rightly directed, not only build into your life anything you want, but remove whatever you do not want. It is the Power of God. It is God Himself. It is the greatest thing in you. It is your highest Self. It is the sum total of all your possibilities, physical, mental and spiritual.

If you have failed to contact this Power through previous efforts; if you have failed to get from it what you want, then it is because you have made only half-hearted demands upon it. You have only scratched the surface of the Great Within of yourself. You have only touched the top layers of your possibilities. You have obtained only partial and fragmentary results because you have not made the supreme demand and the supreme effort.

The ancient invitation is to "Call upon me (God) in the day of trouble," but that call must e backed up with the whole of you. Every whit of you must be there in what you are trying to accomplish. There must be no part of you absent from the call which you make. If you approach your needs from this angle then you can get what you want.

You can get what you want, if you realize that man-power plus God-power is greater than any obstacle that can oppose itself to your will.

If you will change your thought and keep it changed. If you will change it out of the old and keep it changed into the new.

If you will cultivate a consciousness that entertains only constructive and positive thoughts, and refuse to give attention or power to destructive and negative thoughts.

If you will keep your thoughts up to God until they are harmonized with the Creative thought of the Universe.

If you will keep your mind fixed upon the things and conditions you want, so that the Power can work in your behalf.

If you will think of yourself as a son and consciously receive your sonship, so that the Power of God may flow through you.

If you will realize that God and you are inseparable, as Principle and idea, Spirit and identity.

If you will possess yourself in the constructive and affirmative side of good.

If you will "let this Mind be in you, which was also in Christ Jesus."

If you will recognize that your mind *IS* the Power of God.

If you know that the world you live in is mental and not physical.

If you seek the Divine Will instead of your own will.

If you know that you are not dealing with problems, persons, places and things, but with your thoughts about problems, persons, places and things.

If you go to the Inner Power first and use it to the full in all your mental and practical affairs.

If you will make your mind a fortress which evil suggestions besiege in vain.

If you never look outside your consciousness for anything.

If you know always that God is Good and that nothing ever opposes that Good.

If you realize that you never have any responsibility for anything but the thought that is in your mind.

If you realize that good is determined for you and not by you.

If you lay aside all beliefs in two powers, and see only Good.

If you are willing to back up your desire by your whole being, by an all-consuming passion, unbounded enthusiasm and a vision which knows no retreat and acknowledges no failure.

If you are willing to bring your whole self; your whole faith; your unswervable resolution; your greatest efforts; your persistency, your invincibility and your industry to your need.

If you take time every day to commune with God.

If you sincerely strive to live up to your affirmations and prayers every minute of the day.

If you thank God in sincere gratitude for every blessing that comes into your life.

If you look directly to God for everything you need, instead of looking to persons, places, conditions and things.

If you refuse to let outer circumstances disturb your peace of mind and usurp your time and energy.

If you cast all your burdens upon the Lord without dictating and outlining the manner in which His blessings are to come to you.

If you accept your mistakes and failures as opportunities for greater growth.

If you always ask for others the good that you ask for yourself.

If you rejoice in the triumphs, successes and blessings of others without feeling envious of, or inferior or superior to them.

If you have these abilities, plus a strong resolution to apply them to your needs. If you are willing to throw yourself into this study with your entire being, then you will find what you are seeking, and you will accomplish that which you set out to do.

VITAL POINTS IN DEMONSTRATION:

You Can Get What You Want If You Return Home

I
Liberty Under Law

The parable of the Prodigal Son is in reality a lesson on man's relationship to God. In it Jesus is showing that there is a reciprocal action between God's Mind and our minds; that He turns to us as we turn to Him; and that the Spirit will help us and give to us whenever we turn to It. God is both Love and Law. The Love of God is the Father's willingness to give us whatever we need — all we can take; and the Law of God is the means through which we receive.

Jesus first announced this law of cause and effect in His statement that "Whatsoever a man soweth that shall he also reap." This means that we can have only those things which we take through our beliefs. "It is done unto you according to your beliefs." The act of taking from God is three-fold — mental, spiritual and physical. Before we can reach out and take the blessing with the physical hand, we first must inwardly (mentally and spiritually) be receptive to it — accept it in our thought. We must be receptive to it.

Our power of choice enables us to select whatever we want; but ignorance of the law often causes us to choose evil instead of good. Why is this? And why, if we are made in the image and likeness of God, are we able to choose evil as well as good? Because we are individuals and have the power of self-choice. As in the garden of Eden, there always are two possibilities open to man, and he can choose that which he pleases. Evil is not a thing of itself, but a wrong relationship to the law.

11

If we believe in both good and evil then we shall experience some of both — our world will be a mixture of heaven and hell. But if we believe only in the good, then we shall experience only good. This is the Law, and we are all subject to It. "We are the offspring of love, but subject to law."

To understand this famous story of the Prodigal Son as told by Jesus, we must study it in the light of modern psychology and metaphysics. We must keep in mind that the real world according to Jesus is not the visible world; the real world is the invisible, of which the visible is but the form. "Heaven to us may be a dream of earth: but to Him earth was a broken and shadowy reflection of heaven. The material was ordained as a sign language of the spiritual. "For the invisible things of Him since the creation of the world are clearly seen, being perceived through the things that are made, even His everlasting power and divinity."

Like every other story that Jesus told, the parable of the Prodigal Son has two sides — the outer side and the inner side. If we view it only from the physical or objective side, as most people do, then we miss the deeper meanings and lessons which Jesus taught. It will pay us therefore to study this particular parable in light of its psychological and metaphysical implications, and with a firm intention to let its principles germinate within our minds.

Briefly, "psychology is a study of the actions and reactions of thought of the individual mind, and metaphysics is a study of the relationship between this individual mind and the Universal Mind." To the psychologist, for instance, the "two sons" would represent two distinct personalities — the extravert and the introvert, while to the metaphysician they would represent two states of consciousness.

Jesus' statement that "a certain man had two sons" would to the psychologist mean that a certain man had two physical boys — one alienating himself by his sins of passion, and the other alienating himself by his sins of temper. The one eats "the husks of fleshliness"; the other eats the "food of a sour spirit." To the metaphysician, on the other hand, the "two sons" would mean that as a son of God every man has the right of self-choice — he has the possibility of experiencing both good and evil.

The important thing in Jesus' parables always is the inner teaching and we should not, as Chrysostom warned, "Be overbusy about the rest." That is, we should not be too much concerned with the details of the story lest we lose its heart. "Our delight in the parables," says Wernle, "rises regularly in the exact degree in which we succeed in liberating ourselves from the interpretations of the evangelist and yielding ourselves up to the original force of the parables themselves."

If we read the story metaphysically, that is spiritually, and keep in mind Jesus' statement that "God is Spirit: and they that worship Him must worship Him in Spirit and in Truth," then we shall find that there is one main theme setting forth the reciprocal action between the Universal and the individual mind, and several auxiliary themes showing how we can keep in touch with God and draw from Him whatever we need.

The purpose of the parable is eight-fold: to arouse the mind, to awaken the inner power, to bring out the possible man, to deepen the faith, to expand the consciousness, to quicken the will, to intensify the realization of good and to make the principles of the parable operative in our lives.

The Prodigal Son probably is the best known of all the lesser characters in the New Testament. He has been preached about, preached to and preached at more than any one other character in the Bible. He has been denounced for his sins and mistakes, and excoriated for his self-assertion and self-will, condemned for his moral and spiritual bankruptcy, his apostasy of conduct and spendthrift folly. Yet, as George Murray says, "It is the most divinely tender and humanly touching story ever told on our earth."

The story has a message for everyone of us, regardless of our position or station in life, and regardless of how far we may have advanced in Truth. It is a story of Everyman and his journey from sense to soul. According to the old Hebrew priests there were 3,242 things a man had to do in order to be spiritual. According to this parable there is only one — to return to God — to harmonize our minds with His Mind and to surrender our wills to His Will.

And how shall we do this? By bringing ourselves back into line with God's Law of Good. "There is a spirit in man, and the breath of the Almighty giveth them understanding," The Spirit is with us always but to step down the Good (bring it into visibility), God needs our single vision and our undivided allegiance to work through. Religion is not a lot of churches, choirs, schools, denominations, creeds, rites, forms, clergy, restrictions, prohibitions nor fine spun theories. It is a WAY of LIFE individualized, personalized, and practiced by human beings according to their understanding of spiritual Law, the Law of Good.

God IS the Law of Good, the answer to every problem and the fulfillment of every need, and man can put this law into perfect action in his life. He can do it by keeping himself in line with the Law so that it works in his affairs.

This is the Truth Jesus announced when He said, "Ye shall know the truth and the truth shall make you free." Free from what? Free from inharmony, worry, fear, frustration, sickness, problems, difficulties and limitation of every sort. This law exists potentially in the nature of every man, and can be brought into perfect fulfillment through the recognition that he is the son (center of manifestation), where all God's blessings are poured out in abundant measure.

"SON, THOU ART EVER WITH ME AND ALL THAT I HAVE IS THINE." Now pause for a moment until you get the full realization of what that means. As God's son you do not have to get any special favors, divine decrees nor heavenly dispensations to claim what is innately yours. You merely have to recognize who you are (God's son), establish yourself in His Law of Good and press your claim.

Does that sound difficult? Then, it is no more so than when the King of England exercises his power as sovereign of the British Empire. The power vested in the King can be effective only when it is recognized and expressed. But you are a king, too, with an inheritance so rich that the human mind cannot even fathom it. Then why do you have such a hard time getting along, keeping your head and affairs above water and keeping the proverbial wolves from your door? Because you beg instead of claim that which is already yours.

Didn't it ever occur to you that little blessings are harder to get than big ones—not because of God's unwillingness nor any limit of His Power, but by reason of His fabulous wealth. If you turn your faucet on full force and hold a teaspoon under it, you will come and hold a teaspoon under it, you will come away with an empty spoon. Why? Because of too much water. The pressure of the water splashes the contents out because the spoon is too small. And so it is with our poor little prayers and feeble claims upon God's abundance.

Jesus said, "I came that they might have life, and have it more abundantly. "These things have I spoken — that your joy may be made full." "All things whatsoever the Father hath are mind (thine)." "My peace I give unto you." Now ask yourself, "Is my joy full?" "Do I have peace?" "Do I have the same certitude of limitless living that Jesus had?" "Am I free from fear, worry, mental distress, tension, inhibitions and trouble? You can be.

"With God, all things are possible." Do you believe this? Do you believe that there is a Power within you that is greater than any problem in your world? Do you believe that the son of God hath power on earth to forgive sins (correct the mistakes) of the human mind and its thinking? It makes no difference to what church you belong, how many times you make your communion, give of your substance, say your prayers, nor what name you use to designate the mighty Presence of God, if you do not believe in this law of unlimited good and personalize it (set it to working) in your own consciousness, then you cannot hope to share in God's blessings nor receive answers to your prayers.

The scientific way to establish yourself in God's Law of Good is not by talking about what you hope He will do for you, but to act as though it had already been done — to invite His blessings into your consciousness. You are not only to think of God as the only Presence and Power in your life, but you must cooperate with Him in every thought, word, belief, and deed. Thus you set the Law of Good in operation in your life. You harmonize your mind so completely with His Mind that doubt, evil and adverse appearances can no longer prevail against it.

Your own consciousness, of course, must be the proving ground for every truth you wish to build into your life. There are many scriptural statements for accomplishing this but we know of none more effective than the first line of the Twenty-third Psalm: "The Lord is my shepherd; I shall not want"; or the master affirmation: "There is no limitation: for Thou art the Supreme and sole Reality of being, and Thou art the glorious fulfillment of every desire."

Perhaps the greatest stumbling block to those who set out to establish themselves on the affirmative side of Good is the complete change that is required of them in their attitude toward Life. We do not make ourselves centers of the highest manifestation by sending out thoughts and holding feelings that call out the worst in others and from the universe in general, but by radiating the positive elements of love, confidence, harmony and peace, which call out the best.

As we use the good we have we attract more. More power as we generate the power we have. More peace as we express the peace we have. More courage. More faith. More happiness. More Life. More Truth. More substance. More health. Like begets like. Like attracts like. The more of every good thing we express the more it shall increase in our lives.

It is imperative, therefore, that we take an inventory of our attitudes at the earliest possible moment, and that we set about stamping out all attitudes which are inimical to our good. In our return home we are asking God to speed us on our way. We are tired of the husks and pig pens of the world and we want to get home without delay. The desire is all well and good, but we ought to remind ourselves that the process will be accelerated only in proportion as we show our ability to jettison the things which took us away.

We all glory in the One Power of God. But we need to remind ourselves many times that there are two ways of using It, as illustrated by Jesus in His cursing of the fig tree. In this instance, He used the identical power to destroy that He used to heal. He used it in the same way that man uses electricity. The power employed to electrocute a criminal is the same power that we use to make our toast. We are dealing with Law and the Law relates itself to us as we relate ourselves to It. If electricity burns up our house it is not electricity that was at fault but our relation to it. If we, deliberately or in ignorance, live outside the Law of Good then we live contrary to our best interests. Have we then broken the Law? No! We have broken ourselves on the Law.

Probably one of the greatest difficulties in human life today is that too many of us try to change the other fellow. When will we learn that there never is any problem, provocation or situation in life which necessitates our changing someone else? We do not need to try to change others. But only ourselves. The other fellow changes as we change our thought about him. Our blessings increase by appreciation of what we possess. Gratitude keeps our good in circulation. Prayers that depend upon principles will be answered. Those that depend upon persons, places and things will not be answered.

Let us return, then, to the subject of our attitudes and see what should be done about them. In the third paragraph of this chapter, we stated that the power of choice enables us to select whatever we want. We can decide whether we shall be good or bad, true or false, pleasant or mean, happy or sad, positive or negative. Attitudes are creative and they not only affect our own lives, but the lives of those around us. They determine the direction in which we move—up or down, backward or forward. It is a salutary thing at the beginning of a study of this kind, therefore, to discover our basic attitudes and to cancel those which are failing to bring out the best in ourselves and in others. The supreme test of every Truth student is not how much he knows of metaphysics and philosophy, but how much truth he puts to work in his life. Most of us are like the man spoken of in the twelfth chapter of Proverbs: "The slothful man roasteth not that which he took in the hunting; but the previous substance of man is to the diligent." The thrill of the hunt ends with the kill. The preparation and roasting of the game must be left to others. We are more interested in hunting than in what we catch, and this is one of our greatest weaknesses. We love to read books, listen to sermons and lectures, but we do so little about what we learn. "The slothful man roasteth not that which he took in the hunting; but the precious substance of man is to the diligent." The antidote for sloth, then, is diligence, and diligence is defined as an "assiduous and constant application." Indeed, it is the determining factor in every successful achievement.

Prodigals do not always follow the pattern outlined in our story — riotous indulgence ending in pig pens. Prodigality is anything that keeps us from being at our best, doing our best and having the best. It stems from our attitudes and from our failure to develop (use) what we have for the advancement of ourselves and others. The lazy or slothful person is just as much a prodigal as the drunkard or gambler. He who allows his body to become soft and flabby through indifference and love of ease is as much a prodigal as the man who lives in vice and lust. The person who neglects his mind is as much a prodigal as that one who uses it for his own destruction.

In the mind of Jesus there seemed little difference between sins of the body and sins of the mind. In fact, He spent more time excoriating the uncharitableness and selfishness of the Pharisees than He did in denouncing those sins so often associated with the prodigal son.

Let us take inventory of our attitudes, then, to see if we are applying truth to the fullest extent in our every day lives. Let us be absolutely honest in answering the questions that follow; otherwise, we shall learn little from them. The purpose of the test here given is, of course, to discover, and then eliminate all the "prodigal" elements in our minds, and to make our consciousness true and sound to the center. The process is similar to stage effects, where, by the use of lights, certain things are blacked out and others brought forward.

Some of the questions in the test have to do with our personal lives and affairs, and others with the lives and affairs of those around us, but all are pertinent and important in the realization of our final goal, which is to establish ourselves firmly in God's Law of Good. We should, therefore, go over the list every day until we have eliminated everything in our characters and consciousness unlike God and inimical to our good.

We should also remember that what comes into our lives is of the exact nature of some thought, idea, belief or feeling which is lurking somewhere in the inner mind. It is not enough to repeat the affirmation "Nothing but good can come into my life" unless we consciously set about to eliminate every attitude, thought, belief and feeling which keeps it out. In other words, we must keep the good pouring in by letting the evil out.

THE ATTITUDE TEST

1. Am I willing to change conditions by first changing myself?
2. Do I observe all the rules of health and right thinking?
3. Am I at peace with the whole world?
4. Do I accept the responsibility for everything that goes wrong in my life?
5. Do I show good will toward everyone who crosses my path?
6. Am I short or cross with people?
7. Do I always under all circumstances try to see and magnify the good in people?
8. Am I easily upset or annoyed by what others say or do?
9. Do I get moody and depressed when things go wrong?
10. Do I become petulant and irritable when I cannot have my way?
11. Am I easily discouraged when my plans are thwarted or answers are long delayed?
12. Do I secretly cherish grudges and ill-feelings toward others?
13. Do I judge "according to appearances"; am I quick to pass judgment on others?
14. Are my feelings easily hurt and do I quickly take offense?
15. Do I have a mind for trouble, misfortune or symptoms?
16. Do I listen to gossip and syndicate what I hear?
17. Is my tone of voice always cheerful, friendly and helpful?
18. Do I always strive to give my best and be my best under all circumstances?
19. Do I share wholeheartedly and generously with others?

20. Am I patient, tolerant, kind and loving?
21. Am I diligent in the application of Truth to all the problems in my life?
22. When in trouble do I always turn first to God?
23. Do I respond negatively or positively to criticism?
24. Do I resent, argue, nag, criticize or condemn?
25. Do I try to impose my personal will on others?
26. Am I suspicious, jealous, antagonistic or resistant?
27. Am I easily confused, frightened or worried?
28. Am I short-tempered, sensitive, covetous or grasping?
29. Is my mind always receptive to god and free from falsity, taint and other clutter?
30. Do I hold steadfastly to Truth in the face of seeming disaster?
31. Do I love the good in others and ignore the bad?
32. Do I forgive everybody and everything at all times?
33. Do I keep my vision one-pointed and clear?

Keep answering and checking yourself by these questions each day until you have weeded out all the prodigal elements in your character.

You Can Get
What You Want
If You Return Home

II
The Two Sons

The story begins by saying that "A certain man had two sons." The certain man, of course, means God, or the Universal Spirit. In this, as in all His other parables and teachings, Jesus was showing the relationship between God and man, between Universal Mind and the individual mind. He was pointing out that the individual's power and proximity to the Spirit depended largely upon his consciousness of the Divine Presence, and his cooperation with the Law.

He was showing that it is only when man and God are in perfect harmony that man attracts the best things from life. The more intimate a man's relationship with God, the more power will he express, because he draws upon the limitless resources of heaven. So, when Jesus says "A certain man," He means God, the Universal Mind or creative Spirit.

But why did Jesus say that this "certain man" had only two sons? Why did He not say that there were millions of sons, or that every human being was His son? Well, He had two very definite reasons. The first was to show that the relationship between man and God is a relationship of freedom. Man is God's son, but he also is an individual. He has the power of self-choice. He can act on his "own", live on his own, and think or do as he pleases. The second reason was to show that there is but one Power in the Universe — the changeless and unconditional Power of God — and but two ways of using It, either as a son toward God, or as a prodigal toward self.

Life as Jesus taught It is neither good nor bad. It simply is Divine Energy. The energy that is turned into sickness, limitation, suffering and want in no way differs from the energy that finds expression in health, plenty, peace and every other form of good. The difference is not in the power nor in God, but in the thought and will that divert it into constructive or destructive channels. It was Jesus Who taught us that there is but one House and many rooms. "In my Father's house," He said, "are many mansions.

Actually the prodigal son and the older brother were in the same place at the same time. One wastes his substance in riotous living. The other wastes his life in selfish thinking. They were both prodigals in the sense that both were reckless (extravagant) with life. As some one has said, "The attitude of both sons was commercial. The younger son wanted an overdraft; the older brother wanted to open a deposit account." God is not a supernatural banker whose chief business is to pay out money, but a loving Father who daily resurrects, recreates the image of perfection, and supplies human needs.

Thus the difference between the prodigal son and the elder brother was a difference in attitude. Prodigality, as we have already said, is everything (thought, word, feeling or act) that diverts or separates us from the love and power of God.

Most of us spend too much time looking for God and not enough time letting Him find us. We find Him not by looking for Him but looking away from self. We find Him by putting ourselves in the way of being found by Him. That means, stop running away by thinking outside of yourself. If God is Omnipresent (everywhere equally present) and instantly available as Jesus said, then we find Him by recognition and realization. He turns to us as we turn to Him. He finds us when we are absent from ourselves.

The Power always present, but what It does for us and to us depends entirely upon relationship and attitude toward God. It always will be to us what we are to It. That is why Jesus said that there were two sons, and not many. He is talking about two possibilities in everyone's thought and faith. He is talking about you and me as individuals. The son is both free to think as he pleases and do as he chooses. Otherwise he could not exercise a real state of sonship.

The prodigal son did not purposely start out to wreck himself nor to ruin his career. There is no indication that he was a criminal, nor was he abnormal in any way. He was, on the contrary, strangely like you and me. That is what Jesus is bring out — man is an individual and can do as he chooses. He can think what he chooses to think, do what he wants to do and be what he wants to be. It is all up to the individual and the way he uses his mind. He can fill his life with blessings or curses, with desirable things or undesirable things according to the nature and trend of his thought.

If man enters into God then God will enter into him. Then life-time ventures will not end in frustration and defeat, because God and man working together can do things which neither can accomplish alone. In complete unity with God, man will never suffer lack or limitation, because he will be in constant touch with the Source of All-Supply. Man's needs will then be supplied automatically. With his thoughts on God and with the right pattern in his mind, he will head toward his ideals and they will head toward him.

That is what Jesus meant when He said, "I and the Father are one"; and, again, "My Father worketh hitherto, and I work." Man and God working together make an unbeatable combination. When man is God-centered, he not only is assured of success in his undertaking, but he is made immune to the ills of flesh.

III
The Divine Response

"And the younger of them said to his father, Father, give me the portion of goods that falleth to me. And He divided unto them his living."

"Give me the portion of goods that falleth to me." This sounds like a tale of modern times. Conditions at home were irksome; its blessings and freedom imposed restraints. The boy was growing up. He wanted to live his life in his own way. He wanted freedom without restraints. He wanted to live away from home and still enjoy the blessings of home. He wanted to be outside the Kingdom and inside the Kingdom at the same time.

The sullen resentment and jealousy of his brother and the loving discipline and authority of his father annoyed him. Life beckoned. He could hear the call to the heights. Hills were green far away. There were wonderful and fascinating places beyond the narrow confines of home — illusory places — "the primeval lie of liberty without law." Did the Father try to restrain him? Did He attempt to keep him at home? Did He warn him of the error of his way, of the dangers ahead? He did not. Why? Because he was an individual and could do as he pleased, and because "home would not be home to a boy of alien will."

Now, compare the attitude of the Father toward His children with the attitude of human parents toward theirs. "Except a grain of wheat fall into the ground and die, it abideth alone; but if it die, it bringeth forth much fruit." Emilie Cady, in her book "How I Used Truth," says that "Every soul must go down until he strikes his own level, his own self, before there can be any real growth. We may seem to hold another up for awhile, but eventually he must walk alone. The time of his walking alone with his own indwelling Christ, his own true self, will depend largely upon our letting go of him."

No one will seek anything higher than he is today, until he feels the need of something higher. Your dear ones must have the liberty to live out their own lives, and you must let them, or else you are the one who puts off the day of their salvation.

"But," says someone whose heart is aching over the error ways of a loved one, "should you not help anyone? Should you not run after him, and urge him continually to turn into the right way?

"Yes and no. I gladly, joyfully help anyone when he wants help, but I could not urge anyone to leave his own light and walk by my light. Nor would I, like an overfond mother, pick up another and try to carry him in my arms continually 'treating' him.

"A mother may—and sometimes does, mentally, if not physically—through her false conception of love, carry her child until he is twenty years old, lest he, not knowing how to walk, fall and bump his nose a few times. But if she does until he is a grown man, what will he do? He will turn and rend her, because she has stolen him his inherent right to become a strong, self-reliant man. She has interposed herself between him and the power within him which was waiting from his birth, to be strength and sufficiency for him in all things. She should have placed him on his own feet, made him know that there was something within himself that could stand, encouraged and steadied him, and so helped him to be self-reliant and independent.

"Hundreds of anxious fathers and mothers, sisters and wives say, 'Ah! but I love this one so I cannot stand still and see him rushing on to an inevitable suffering.'

"Yes, you love him. But I tell you that it takes an infinitely greater, more Godlike love to stand still and see your child burn his hand a little, that he may gain self-knowledge, than it does to be a bondslave to him, ever on the alert to prevent the possibility of his learning through a little suffering. Are you equal to this larger love — to the love which does not hold itself on the qui vive to interpose its nagging bodily presence between the dear ones and their own indwelling Lord who is 'with them always'? Having come yourself to the mighty truth that 'God is all in all,' have you the moral courage to 'be still know'; to take off all restrictions and rules from others, and to let the God within them, each one, grow them as He will; and trusting Him to do it in the right way, keep yourself from all anxiety in the matter.

"It is written, 'Whose soever sins ye remit, they are remitted unto him; and whose soever sins ye retain, they are retained.' Will you invariably speak the word of remission or loosing to your erring ones. Or will you bind them closer, tighter, in the bondage which is breaking your own heart, by speaking the word of retention to them continually?

"If you really want your friends to be free, there is but one way for you: Loose them and let them go. For it is the promise of the Father, through the Son, that 'whatsoever ye loose on earth shall be loosed in Heaven'."

That is one of the great lessons in our story: No one has the right to coerce another to accept his ideal. Every person has a right to keep his own ideal until he desires to change it.

"God is leading your friend by a way you do not and cannot know. It is a safe and sure way; it is the shortest and only way. It is the Christ way; the within way.

"But," you say, "is there nothing I can do when I see my husband, brother, friend going down?"

"Yes, there is something you can do, and a very effectual something, too.

" 'The sword of the Spirit is the word.' You can, whenever you think of your friend, speak the word of freedom to him. You can always and in all ways 'Loose him, and let him go, not forgetting that the letting him go is as important as the loosing him. You can tell him mentally that Christ lives within him, and makes him free; tell him that he manifests the Holy One wherever he goes and at all times, for there is nothing else to manifest. And then you see to it that you do not recognize any other manifestation than good in him."

"He divided unto them his living." That is another striking thing about this story—God's instant response to the son's request. When he asked for his share of the family fortune, God gave it to him. He did not argue. Why not? Because argument implies an opposite and God has no opposite. "We argue to arrive at a correct conclusion. God already is the correct conclusion of all things, therefore He does not need to argue." The Father did not argue with him, nor try to change his mind or restrain him in any way. He did not ask him what he was going to do with the money—whether he was going to buy a horse, an automobile, or stocks or bonds. "He divided unto them his living."

The son asked for what he wanted and the Father gave it to him. There were no questions asked, no papers to fill out. There were no restrictions, no limitations and no interest. "The Universe gives us what we ask; experience alone will teach us what is best for us to have." As long as the younger son was in the Father's House (God Consciousness) he could have what he wanted, by the simple process of taking it — using what was already there. And so it is with us.

Material things will always come to us when we have the belief or mental equivalent of what we ask. God has something higher and greater for us than money, automobiles, houses, fine clothes and lands. "Eye hath not seen, nor ear heard, neither hath it entered into the heart of man, the things that He hath prepared for them that love him" — What? Material possessions? Personal Power? Bank accounts? Stocks and bonds? No, "that love Him" — that love Truth for Truth's sake, that love God more than self. Jesus said: "They that have forsaken houses . . . or lands, for My name's sake shall receive an hundred fold now in this time of houses . . . and lands."

"Give me the portion of goods that falleth to me." There are many lessons tucked away in this portion of the story, but probably none more important than the implied frustration which one reads so easily into the lines. The younger son had come to the end of his rope. He was "fed up." He had taken all he could and he was now going to strike out for himself. He was going to do great things and without the help of anyone else. All he wanted was a grub-stake and he would change everything in his world.

What a familiar ring this part of the story has. If things were just different where I am. If I could just get away some place. If I could just get away from so and so, or such and such, then everything would be alright, etc, etc. Yes, it is the old belief that hills are greener far away, or what modern psychiatrists would call just plain frustration. Either your problem is too big for you or you are too small for your problem. You have your "castles in Spain" but others are standing in your way. You cannot be successful where you are, because competition is too keen. Conditions always seem more favorable in some other place, opportunities always seem greater. You have a big deal that would make you rich but you do not have what it takes to put it over.

Prosperity is always around the corner but you never run into it. Why not? Because you do not have an integrated mind. You are trying to work from the circumference instead of from the center. You are working without power because you have not harnessed your power with God-Power. You have lost your centrality. You are trying to live your life on the low levels of conscious thinking and you are diverting life instead of unifying it. You are scattering your good instead of attracting it. You are scattering your good instead of attracting it. may be you should read again the summary of the law. The solution lies in organization — keeping your whole being (body, mind and soul) centered in God.

When Jesus said, "He that findest his life shall lose it, but he that loseth his life for my sake shall find it," He did not mean that we had to die in order to find God or Heaven. He meant that we had to leave the consciousness of self and enter the Consciousness of Christ. The clear command is: "Let this Mind be in you, which was also in Christ Jesus." Just as there are two periods in the measurement of time, B. C. and A. D., before Christ and after Christ, so there are two periods in the life of every man — the government of self and the government of God.

That is why Jesus told Nicodemus that he must be born again. But "How can a man be born again when he is old?" asked Nicodemus. Now listen to Jesus' reply: "Except a man be born again of water (i.e. baptized), and of the spirit (i.e. renewed in the spirit of his mind), he cannot enter the Kingdom of God."

To become God-centered and God-directed is not something difficult or hard to understand. It is simply a change of identity and a reversal of thought. Instead of keeping self at the center of consciousness as in the past, we now put God there and organize our life around Him. Jesus said, "Judge not according to appearances, but judge righteous judgment." In other words, do not accept or evaluate things as they appear, but look past the appearance to the Reality back of them.

The self-centered person lives in a house of mirrors. No matter where he looks he never sees anything but himself. No matter where he goes he always runs into himself. Now, let us suppose that this same person suddenly discovers something within himself that is other than and greater than himself, and let us suppose that he begins to think and act as though this other self were his Real or True Self. What happens to the mirrors? They become windows through which he looks," not at himself but beyond himself" to God and the Good that is at hand.

Someone has likened ego-centricity (self-centeredness) "to an internal infection, located so deep in our system that no operation can be performed." The infection, to use a popular expression, has to be drawn out. Centering our attention in God and practicing His Presence, "acts like a spiritual mustard plaster, drawing us out of ourselves and opening" our whole being to God, to such an extent "that our diseased self will come to the surface and be healed by the warm rays of the Divine Son."

When Emerson said that "Self-consciousness is the fall of man," he meant that self-centeredness is the breeding place of all sickness, misery, trouble, sorrow, insecurity, fear, worry, limitation and defeat. Then what is the cure for such a deadly disease? The answer is: Become God-centered, or, as St. Paul said, "Put off the old man and put on the new man, which is Christ." The basic principle on which all spiritual promises are fulfilled, as Jesus pointed out is absolute selflessness and obedience to the Will of God. Thus, to become God-centered or selfless one must forsake (lose) the personal sense of life and embody the Christ, or Spiritual Idea of life. In other words, he must remove the cause of all his trouble (excessive concern with his own personality) before he can remove the trouble.

And how does one do that? By thinking of God and others, and not only thinking about others, but by becoming interested in them and doing something for them. And when will the cure begin? When you have started doing something about what you have just read.

But maybe you are one of those troubled souls who feel insecure in a fickle and dangerous world. You are worried about the future, and what is going to happen to your possessions and to you. When you were young your future seemed secure. Your parents or others provided for your education, insurance and a comfortable future. Then, in the twinkling of an eye, the future became dark. You were thrown back upon your own resources pretty much as was the prodigal son in the far country. Your material security vanished and you found that you were bounded on four sides by yourself. What could you do? Where could you turn? But two ways seemed open to you — up or down.

To the materially-minded, such a debacle will seem most terrifying — a calamity — lives shattered because of it. To the spiritually-minded, on the other hand, it will appear as a blessing — just as God would have it. The spiritually-minded will see in it the working out of Divine Will, throwing people back on the Infinite Resource of supply and making them self-reliant — instead of trusting in the false security of material things, they now will be compelled to find their security in God. "Now is the accepted time," said Jesus; "now is the day of salvation." Perhaps that is one of the great lessons the world is to learn — that the only real future is in God and that there is no permanence in things.

The only time Spirit knows is the Eternal NOW, and the only permanent riches are spiritual Ideas. When we finally settle down to that we shall discover, as Jesus said, that the only security, here or hereafter, is to be found in the riches. (possessions) of the mind. "Lay not up for yourselves treasures upon earth, where moth and rust do corrupt or thieves break through and steal, but lay up for yourselves treasures in heaven (mind) which are eternal." Spiritual Ideas, which are our only support, come to us not because of an abundance of material possessions, or the lack of them, but because of the receptivity we show toward God. When we possess that receptivity we shall have a security that nothing in the world can take from us, or even shake.

"Wilt thou be made whole?" Will God forgive your sins, cure your ills and supply your needs? He certainly will. When? When you return home (become God-centered), and commit your will to His Will and your mind to His Mind. Only thus can you share again in the enduring satisfactions and abiding security of the Father's House.

IV
The Good Always Is in Manifestation

"He divided unto them his living"

Probably the most common mistake we humans make in spiritual work is the unfortunate habit of postponing our good until some future time. "When I get my new position, I'll be the happiest person in the world," says one. Another says, "I'll be so happy when my bills are paid"; "When this law suit is settled"; "When I get on my feet again"; "When we get married"; "When we get our new house"; "When I get well."

These are just a few of the attitudes which postpone our good, and the unfortunate part of it is that we live constantly in a suspended state of happiness and incompletion. When our goal is reached then we again begin to postpone our happiness until another has been attained.

Of course, it is right and proper that we rejoice when our objectives have been attained, but it is not right that we should be unhappy while waiting to attain them. Jesus said that "the Kingdom of Heaven is at hand." What did He mean? He meant that the good we seek always is in manifestation and always ready for our use, but that we must be in the Father's House (harmonized with His Mind) in order to obtain it.

The time to be happy is right now. "Now is the acceptable time." The stuff that blessings are made of is here now. It is all about us — in the very air that we breathe. It is within our consciousness awaiting our command. It will come forth into expression whenever we give it the opportunity, whenever we are in unity with God. "God is a very present help in trouble."

The divine response is not dependent on time, circumstances or conditions, but upon our faith, recognition, realization, attitudes, thoughts and words. Since happiness is a state of being and not of having, then we can be happy wherever we are and in whatever circumstances we find ourselves.

When Jesus told us to "Seek first the Kingdom of God," He meant that we were to recognize it, realize it, deserve it, and live in it. The kingdom of God cannot be won by achievement any more than can the air which we breathe. It must be accepted by recognition, realization and conformity to its laws. It is a way of life, a way of thinking, acting and living. It is our awareness and receptivity toward God in and through all the vicissitudes of our daily life. We think of the prodigal son as the extravert and the elder brother as the introvert, but the ideal development as pointed out by Jesus is the ambivert or balance between the two. The ambivert is the "receptive-positive," the inlet outlet type.

In His sermon on the Mount, Jesus said of one group, "The Kingdom of Heaven is theirs." What did He mean? He meant that these people had not only found the place and manner in which God dispenses His blessings, but that they had vitally attuned themselves to It. Like the lump of leaven hidden in the three measures of meal, they had centered themselves in It. And who were these people? They were the receptive and the positive — the inlets and outlets of all that there is in God. They no longer belonged to the Kingdom but the Kingdom of God belonged to them. They had It in the possessive case. Its powers were in them, through them, around them, beneath them, above them, at their disposal. They were in It and It was in them. It was a present fact.

God's Kingdom does not belong to any one church sect or creed, but to the God-centered and one-pointed. As Dana Gatlin says, It "is simply a matter of our awareness of Him as ever present. We must be born anew into spiritual awareness. My individual 'kingdom' is simply a matter of how much, how widely, how intimately I believe in God . . . . It is determined by my conviction of God's never-failing Presence, regardless of what may be happening in the world about me."

One of the first things the author learned in studying about electrical power was that the current of electricity travels in a circuit. As long as the circuit is not broken the power can be appropriated for our needs, but when the circuit is broken the power stops. When we turn the wall switch we complete the circuit, or break it. When we complete the circuit the room is filled with light and when we break it the room is filled with darkness.

"What is the current?" It is the path of the electricity as it flows from the generator at the power plant, and over the city and back to the generator again, which is a part of the circuit. The circuit that you complete, or break, is a part of a greater circuit feeding all the little branches in the homes of the vicinity. What do you do to the circuit in your house affects only your particular lights or electrical appliances. In order to serve you the current of electricity that goes through your wires it must not be prevented from returning to the big generator in the power plant.

"There are two kinds of currents: one is known as D.C. (direct current) and the other as A.C. (alternating current). The direct current flows one way through the circuit; and the alternating current flows first one way, then reverses and flows the other way in the circuit. This change is made very rapidly. In a sixty-cycle current this change occurs sixty times a second. You can understand how rapidly the current travels in order to traverse the many miles of wire serving thousands of homes sixty times every second. It seems like a miracle and it is a miracle."

But let us think for a moment of another power which is even greater than the power of electricity and the Father of it. When Jesus illustrated the movements of Spiritual Power through the lives and thoughts of men He used the symbol of the vine and the branches. "I am the Vine," He said, "ye are the branches: He that abideth in me, and I in him, the same beareth much fruit: for apart from me ye can do nothing." The Vine, of course, is the circuit and the branches are God's children.

God generates the Spirit of life, love, power, health, happiness and supply, and these flow in one mighty current from the Universal Mind through the individual mind and return again to God.

Then why don't we enjoy a constant stream of good in our lives, and why are we beset so much with evil and other forms of ill? Because we have broken our circuit with God and shut ourselves off from His Good. The current of electricity is flowing through the wires constantly, but to get light or power we must plug it in. We must make a connection. So you see now what Jesus meant when He said that "Apart from me ye can do nothing?" The Spirit of Good is flowing through us at all times but to get the good in manifestation (to experience it) we must complete the circuit. To be supplied from the Source we must stay on the Vine. We must keep our thoughts on God.

The circuit is broken through negative thoughts and attitudes, through doubt, fear, anxiety and worry, and it is established again through faith and prayer. When we divide our thoughts between good and evil, we loosen our connections with God and short-circuit His Power. We tighten and open them again through unity and faith. To increase the flow of power we must increase our consciousness of His presence. We must get a firmer connection with our source. And how do we do that? By meditation upon affirmations of Truth.

It is a law that power always flows from the higher potential to the lower. As we keep our thoughts lifted up to God we not only bring the Power of the Infinite into expression, but we cause It to work in our behalf for the things we want. Whatever is weak will be strengthened, and whatever is missing will be supplied. The promise is, that "Though your sins be as scarlet, they shall be as white as snow." The destruction caused by wrong thinking will be avoided and the bad effects of previous wrong thinking will be washed away.

If we keep our thoughts stayed on God, then, no matter what the problem or apparent limitation may be we are delivered and supplied day by day.

The reason many fail in prayer is because their heaven is so widely separated from their needs. There is so much distance (lack of unity) between them that God never gets into their lives. Like the electric current that is not tapped, God's blessings flow right through them on the Divine Circuit and return again to their Source. "Apart from me ye can do nothing." If the space between the prayer and the answer is filled with doubt and speculation, then the consciousness becomes an opacity through which heavenly gifts cannot pass. Without heaven (realization of fulfillment) nothing is possible to us. With Heaven everything is possible.

Jesus sensed this incongruity and separation in man's thought and that is why He taught us to pray "Thy Kingdom come on earth as it is in Heaven." This means literally help me to complete the Divine Circuit. Help me to eliminate from my mind the sense of space (separation) between my life and the Source of all life, between my mind and God's Mind. Help me to realize that the Divine Circuit flowing from God includes me. If there are loose connections in the spiritual circuit they can be tightened by the faithful use of Jesus' affirmation: "Not my will but Thine be done."

When Jesus said that His Kingdom was not of this world, He meant that Heaven (wholeness) could not be realized in a material, or world consciousness. "Spiritual things are spiritually discerned." "As we have borne the image of the earthy, we shall also bear the image of the heavenly." "Like attracts like." To live in Heaven and enjoy its blessings on earth we must have the consciousness of Heaven. We must change our consciousness from matter to Spirit, from self to God.

Since God is omnipresent — everywhere at the same time, then there is no distance between man and God but man's lack of awareness. Heaven is where we are only we don't know it. That is why Jesus, said, "Seek ye first the Kingdom of God." Wake up to It. Become conscious of It. Step It down to your actual needs. "Lo, I am with you always, even unto the end of the world." The distance between earth and Heaven, between the without and the within, between the self and God is not a matter of miles but of consciousness. It is a lack of faith, a lack of awareness.

God serves us in the same way that the electrical generator supplies the light and power needs of our homes. In the Father's House we are in touch with Omnipotence and have unrestricted access to the Fountain Head of all supply. Then how shall we transform, or step down, the Power to our actual needs? By contemplation—creating the forms through which it may become expressed. "If ye continue in my word, then are ye my disciples indeed; and ye shall know the Truth, and the Truth shall make you free."

All we have to do is to recognize the supply, make our demand upon It (take the right patterns into our mind). Believe it, accept it, thank God for it and let it manifest. "If thou return to the Almighty, thou shalt be built up." By keeping our thoughts on God, a power greater than our own works in our behalf. It doesn't make any difference how great the problem, how complex the difficulty, nor how hopeless the case, all things work together for good to those who keep their thoughts stayed on God.

That is the next great revelation in this story. God does not argue nor withhold from man. Man does all the arguing and withholding from himself. "God giveth to all men liberally, and upbraideth not." That is the lesson Jesus is bringing out. God takes every man exactly as he is and asks no questions. He accepts him at his own evaluation of himself and responds to him by corresponding to his new states of mind. The prodigal son received exactly what he asked for. God gave him what he believed was his, no more and certainly no less. His measure of acceptance was filled from the Universal storehouse and he could do with it as he pleased.

That is why the ancients represented the Universe and man's relation to It as a great mirror reflecting back to him what he held before it. The important thing in spiritual work as in anything else is not what a man has or says, but what he is, his Spirit. "For what shall it profit a man, if he shall gain the whole world, and lose his own soul." The vital thing in life is not where we are nor what we may be doing, but are we moving in the right direction. Are we thinking and working with God or with self. "This is life eternal, to know Thee the only true God, and Jesus Christ Whom Thou has sent."

The affirmative factor in successful living is not how much a man knows, but is he using his knowledge toward constructive ends. If the Kingdom of God is within us, as Jesus said, then its appearance on earth depends upon the inner Spirit not upon the outer man.

In the realm of nature the principle of life is very similar to the principle of electricity. The principle of electricity doesn't argue, or · reason, or withhold. It doesn't ask what you are going to use it for. You say, "Electricity, be power," and it is power; "Electricity, be light," and it is light. You say, "Electricity, run the vacuum cleaner, toast the bread, boil the coffee," and it complies. Like the law of life, electricity works the way you choose to use it. It flows into any channel you provide for it.

Jesus understood this perfectly and that is why He told us to seek first the Kingdom of God. Were He here in the flesh today He probably would say: "Make your contact with God first. Complete the circuit before you try to use the Power. Lay hold on Life." In other words, get the power first. Make a firm connection with the inner Source of Supply and things will be added in a surprisingly quick and easy manner.

Thousands pray for the fulfillment of their desires. Thousands pray for healing, supply, happiness and the right solution of their problems, but nothing happens. Why not? Because they have not established themselves in God's Law of Good. They have not sought the Kingdom (power) first; and without power (a completed circuit) the prayer cannot be answered. "As many as RECEIVED Him, to them gave He Power."

"The consciousness of the Absolute (Heaven) will produce emancipation from mental or physical ills, the reason being that there are no ills in the Absolute, and it is not possible for the mind to be conscious of ills when it is in the consciousness of that which is absolutely free from ills. In other words, the mind cannot be in darkness, weakness or disease when it is in light, power and health."

Jesus said, "Whatsoever things ye desire, when ye pray, believe that ye receive them, and ye shall have them." Now, notice the words "Whatsoever things ye desire." Desire, according to Webster, "is a conscious impulse or movement toward an object." If you have an *all-consuming* desire in your heart, and by all-consuming we mean being integrated with God; if it is strong enough to unite your whole personality in one objective, then it will move toward its goal and carry you along with it.

But please notice that a desire is vastly different from a wish. A wish is a desire without power, without action, without effort, without roots. It accomplishes nothing because it attempts nothing. It is not integrated with God. It does not enter the Absolute. It does not draw God to the center of consciousness. That is why people who only wish and hope live in a constant state of delay, disappointment and defeat.

Do you see why it is imperative for you to seek the Kingdom of God first? Do you see what Jesus meant for you to do? It was to align yourself with the glorious power of God, so that you could move with the current instead of against it, so that It could work for you instead of against you. It was to remove all resistance and hindrance from your path.

Yes, my friend, this is the same power that says, "Cast your burden upon the Lord, and He shall sustain thee." Keep your thoughts stayed on God. Keep your desire alive with faith, and no matter what the difficulty or lack may be it will be met. "Thou shalt love the Lord thy God with all thy heart." If you can unite all your faculties in one focal point of desire, so that the whole personality is integrated in the one objective, then you can accomplish anything you set out to do.

It is amazing how many Truth students still think of prayer as a means of getting God to do what they want done. But the very though is fallacious and contrary to the laws of Spirit. No! Prayer is not a means of getting God to do our bidding but of letting Him have His way in us. Theology has confused as in such maters but it is wrong. "Religion is not an option about God; it is an experience with God."

It doesn't make any difference what form of religion a person may follow, the only way he can appropriate God's blessing is through his realization that "the Kingdom of God is within" him, and that it is "at hand." Jesus said, "It is your Father's good pleasure to give you the Kingdom." Then why don't you accept it and make it your own? Why don't you live in It and enjoy its blessings now?

Can it be that your prayers are at fault, that they lack those positive, dynamic qualities which give them character and worth? Then do something about them. Lift them to a higher level of efficiency. "True prayer is not a matter of saying something with our lips. It is a matter of feeling something with our heart — of knowing something with our understanding — of looking with confident expectation for a response, a result."

"Jesus, you remember, made a comparison of two men who prayed. One was a Pharisee who offered a lengthy, ritualistic prayer. The other was a penitent man whose only prayer was, 'God, be merciful to me a sinner.' The latter prayer was approved by the Master. The Pharisee's prayer was mere words; that of the penitent man was charged with meaning" and power.

The starter of a man's car failed to respond when he pushed the button. The service man at the corner was appealed to. "Your battery is dead," was the diagnosis; and he took it out and put in a live one. "But the battery is all right, isn't it?" anxiously inquired the owner, "Absolutely," the battery man assured him. "It's just as good as the loaner I've put in. It's dead, that's all."

"The two batteries looked exactly alike. Yet, while one was charged with power and produced results, the other was dead and, therefore, worthless for all practical purposes. So, too, with a prayer. Used by one person it may accomplish little or nothing. Used by another, it may accomplish a miracle. The reason for this is that in one instance the prayer is like the 'dead' battery — devoid of power, while in the other instance it has been charged, filled, saturated with those essential elements that give life to our words."

That is what Jesus is bringing out in this parable. When a person leaves the Father's House, he is divided house and without power. He is divided between Good and self, between his Higher and his lower nature. The personality is shut off from God and is dead like the car battery. That is why Jesus said to the people with divided loyalties, "No man can serve tow masters. . . . Ye cannot server God and mammon."

There is nothing unusual or strange about this union of man-power with God-power, yet it is the secret way to all spiritual attainment, to answered prayer. This union can be accomplished by any one willing to go all the way, willing to change his consciousness in order to get it. "I and the Father are one." Change your consciousness and your mind and God's Mind come together like water and wine in the chalice of a new consciousness, a consciousness of supply, domination and power. The moment you discover that the power of God is the power of your own mind, that moment you can have most anything you desire. Then your desires will be supplied automatically by virtue of your position in the law.

What do we mean, then, by right desire? We mean anything that is spiritually legal, or that is for our highest good. To get material things we must not only be established in God's Law of Good, but we must have the spiritual prototypes. We must have them in consciousness. St. Thomas Acquinas said, "It is difficult to pray because it is difficult to know what we ought to desire." How, then, may we overcome this difficulty? By first asking God what we ought to desire. Jesus understood the danger of desiring the wrong things, and that is why He warned us to "Seek first the Kingdom of God," and to lay up treasures in Heaven (mind). Since Heaven is where God is, and since it is within you, then it is the starting point of every demonstration.

Do you long for a natural association with your loved ones now in the spiritual body? Then be close to God. Those who were with you on earth can now be close to you in silent prayer. They can even be nearer to you than when they were in the flesh; "but first you must be close to God."

One of the saddest spectacles in life is the man or woman who, after years of indifference and neglect, and with no spiritual resources to fall back upon, suddenly tries to gain faith and courage to meet some great crisis or sorrow. They run feverishly from one thing to another, but nothing seems to give the relief they seek. They are like a man in a life-boat in the middle of the ocean. They have developed nothing permanent in their souls and there is nothing to buoy them up, to see them through.

These bewildered people have not taken trouble to let God into their lives and now they do not know to bring Him out. They have spent their time accumulating treasures on earth and neglected storing up treasures in Heaven.

But may be you do not understand the meaning of Jesus' command to "lay up for yourselves treasures in Heaven." It means to enter into and share Christ's quality of life it means embodying God's thoughts and words within yourself — to make them your own. Right desires are spiritual attributes — Heaven, life, love, power, Truth, wholeness, faith, joy, peace, freedom, happiness, understanding, knowledge, grace and substance.

To lay up treasures in Heaven means to keep your mind in ascendancy, to keep your mental level so high that your thoughts harmonize with the thoughts of God. It means to live so close to God that your whole life, body, soul and Spirit are brought into perfect harmony with Him. "As many as RECEIVED Him, to them gave He power." Be continually raising your thoughts to God, you open yourself to great spiritual power and to a constant stream of good.

And, by the same token, when you lower your mental level you shut off the power and open yourself to destructive forces and to the inflow of a constant stream of evil. The reason good thoughts call out the good and evil thoughts bring the bad, is because good has an affinity for good and bad has an affinity for bad. Both are obedient to a law that is as exact as the law of mathematics.

Few people realize it, but praying can be dangerous. It is dangerous when based on wrong desire. Indeed, desire is the prayer itself. Lives have been ruined because wrong desires (prayers) have been fulfilled. However, we can always meet this danger by desiring the Kingdom of God. Why? Because this is the supreme desire to which every needed thing is added. To attract the best, we must be in tune with God — our request must be spiritually legal and our minds and purpose must lie parallel with His.

One reason many people do not get relief in time of trouble is because they allow to worry and fear to cancel out their higher consciousness of Truth. They try to make important decisions and solve difficult problems while their minds are confused, while they are anxious, apprehensive or fearful. Therefore, never act or make a decision when under pressure, in doubt or when in confusion. Always wait at least twelve hours before thinking out any uncertain problems that comes into your life.

"When thou art cast down say there shall be a lifting up" (Old Testament). When a man's metal level is low can no more do good work spiritually *"than a watch can keep good time when there is friction in the bearings of its delicate mechanism. In order to keep perfect time, the watch must be exquisitely adjusted. Every wheel, every cog, every bearing, every jewel must be mechanically perfect, for any defect, any trouble, any friction anywhere will make absolutely correct time impossible." And what is true of the watch is even more true of the delicate machinery of the mind. It, too, needs regulating and tuning up to its center in prayer every day, and especially so before beginning an important piece of work.

If you have ever watched a centrifugal wringer in a laundry, you have a pretty good picture of the human mind before and after it has been tuned to God.[1] It wobbles so badly when it first begins to revolve that it seems as though it would tear itself to pieces, but gradually, as the velocity increases, the motion becomes steadier and steadier, and the machine speeds with lightning- like rapidity on its center. When it once gains its perfect balance nothing seems to disturb it, although when it first began to revolve the least thing made it wobble."

The problems and difficulties which so easily disturb and frustrate the self-centered man do not in the least affect the confident, God-centered soul. Even great disasters and calamities fail to throw him off center, because he has found his balance in God. He is like the mighty iceberg in the North Atlantic lanes, balanced by an infinite calm in the great undercurrents of the sea. The iceberg is unaffected by the fury of the winds and storms which beat against it, because it is carried along by a power not its own. It rides calmly into gales because its bulk is centered in the mighty depths below.

---

[1] The Miracle of Right Thought, by Orison Swett Marden.

Jesus does not tell us why the younger son left home but there is every indication that it was due to the churlish attitude of his bad-tempered brother. There was inharmony in his thought, and no man can be successful or happy when he is in conflict with himself. Instead of meeting the condition where he was, and as he eventually would have to do, he ran away. He would follow the line of least resistance. He would leave home.

This is an important point in the story because it points out a weakness common to us all. The important thing in dealing with discordant conditions and people is not their attitude towards us, but our attitude toward them. It is a common failing when things do not go to suit us, when conditions fret and annoy, when others do not measure up to our ideas, or when they try to take advantage of us, to "tell them off" or run away. We run away from persons and conditions because we do not realize that they are the embodiment of our thoughts and that every one of them conforms to some belief which we have held concerning them.

"I'm not big enough," said a man who had allowed his life to be thrown out of gear by petty annoyances, "or those things wouldn't hurt me." One of the inescapable proofs of our unity with God is our ability to get along with other people—all people." "He that loveth not his brother whom he hath seen, how can he love God Whom he hath not see."

Dr. Link, in his book, The Return to Religion, says "that the individuals who believed in religion or attended a church had significantly better personalities than those who did not." This is very interesting but we cannot help thinking how much better the personalities of these same people would be if they only practiced the religion they profess; of the superior ability they would have, not only in dealing with others but in dealing with their own personal problems.

We must stop liking people merely for what they do for us and stop disliking them for what they do not do. We must learn to separate the sin from the sinner. Simply because a person says or does something we do not like does not mean we dislike that person, but rather that which he says or does. If we were bigger than what others say about us, then we would not be affected by them.

Jesus did not judge people by what appeared on the surface, by their dispositions or unruly natures. He got inside them and turned them into friends. He took most unpromising people and discovered in them what others did not believe was there. He made them so conscious of their larger selves that little self was scarcely recognizable. As Hugh Black said, "He ever took men on their strongest side. He accepted the highest in them as representing their true self. In the company of sinners he dreamed of saints."

The reason some of our most difficult problems arise from strained relationships with people with whom we live and work, is because of our spiritual immaturity. We do not practice the Truth we know. We do not apply our religion to our needs. It is so much easier to resist an enemy than to pray for him. It is so much easier to condemn an neighbor than to love him "as thyself." It is so much easier to criticize others than to do unto them "as you would have them do unto you." It is so much easier to strike back than to "turn the other cheek."

Most of us believe in God at 11:15 Sunday morning when we say the Creed, but when someone slanders us on Monday, or gets in our way or receives credit for what we do, we become angry and forget all about God. Our spiritual support is gone and we are back on our own. Longfellow said: "The talent of success is nothing more than doing what you call well, and doing well whatever you do without thought of fame." When Jesus did some mighty work, He told His disciples to go and tell no man. "The quickest way for you to destroy the good you have done is to advertise it."

It is obvious, therefore, that the only satisfactory way to change the unpleasant conditions in our environment and to heal the strained relationships in our corporate life, is to change our attitude toward them. Instead of "flying off the handle," chafing or offering resistance, when things go wrong, it would be far saner to sit down within our divided selves and meditate upon some such statement as this: "GOD IN ME MAINTAINS THE HARMONY OF MY BEING." Say it over and over again until harmony, order and peace have been restored.

The reason the deep sea diver is successful in his work under water it because there is within the diving bell a pressure greater than the pressure of the water at the bottom of the sea. "Ye do not need to fight." St. John said: "Greater is He that is in you than he that is in the world."

When you have a spiritual pressure in your consciousness which is greater than the conditions of the outer world, then you will not have to contend with persons and problems, but you can let God work them out for you. You will be like the stone fence, so broad that when it blew over it was as high as it was before. The God-centered person is like that. He does not get upset over untoward settings but turns them into doors. "Stand still, and see the salvation of the Lord."

Spiritual pressure grows through your realization that God is the only presence and power in your life.

The twelve rules for corporate living are:

1. Do not try to dominate others.
2. Do not try to use them.
3. Learn how to put yourself in the other fellow's place.
4. Do not look for perfection in others.
5. Respond to others not as they appear, but as they can be.
6. Meet all misunderstandings and difficulties as they arise — do not let them crystallize.
7. Refuse to look for slights and refuse to be slighted. You always will find what you are looking for.
8. Stop trying to make people over; only God can do that.
9. Look for the best in people rather than the worst. Appeal to the best and the best will come back to you.
10. Make it easy for others to cancel their obligations to you.
11. Take no thought about who gets the credit for what is done.
12. See no evil, hear no evil, speak no evil.

One of the few times during His earthly ministry that Jesus expressed amazement was when the disciples told Him that the devil was coming and suggested that He run. He was amazed, not because of their imagined danger, but because of their imagined danger, but because of their failure to perceive and understand what He had been teaching. When Jesus said "Resist not evil." He did not mean that we should enter into evil, but that resistance was the wrong way to meet it. He knew that evil was nothing but the absence of good; and

He knew that resistance, being a negative quality, could not overcome another negative quality.

Just as the mechanical friction of a dry axle will wear out the axle and wreck the train, so mental friction will wear out the man and wreck his body. To resist evil in the outer world is to create friction in the inner world. If you resist conditions, persons or things, then the friction will be felt as congestion in your body. It will attack your weakest spots and tie your bodily organs in knots, — prevent the harmonious operation of your bodily functions.

Active dislike, dissension, dissatisfaction — all resistant attitudes, will not only develop knots in your muscles and short-circuit your nerves, but they also will create bottlenecks in your affairs. Such congestion, however, can be broken by changing your mental attitude.

Jesus knew that only those things which existed in the within could be objectified in the without. This is true of both evil and good, of the desirable and the undesirable. We need not fear evil in the outer world unless there first is some evil in the inner world. Jesus never compromised with evil, but recognized only the good. "The prince of this world (evil) cometh," He said, "and he hath nothing in me." Since there was no evil in His consciousness, He had nothing to fear in the outer world.

The effective way to change the objectifications of evil in our experience, then, is to change the subjective cause in our consciousness. Since the things that exists within us are the things we always attract to ourselves, the way to get rid of evil conditions in our environment is to get rid of the evil conditions in our minds. We must look for the good only.

The three great sources of friction in the consciousness are resistance, dissatisfaction and dislike. Adults dislike their work, persons, places, conditions and things. Children dislike their teachers, tasks and subjects assigned them at school. Everywhere we find round pegs in square holes, misfits and maladjustments, people wearing themselves out doing things, going places and working with people they dislike. They think it is their responsibilities and the demands others make on them that is wearing them out, but actually it is their own attitude toward them. They excuse their lack of harmony by laying the blame on conditions, other persons or things. Everybody is out of steps but themselves. This is because they do not like to admit their faults.

The college boy who dislikes trigonometry will tell you that it is the most difficult subject in the world. He will tell you that he hates "math," but this is because it is hard for him. Why is it hard for him? Because he does not understand it and because he dislikes, it. The trouble is not in trigonometry but in himself. When he under stands it it will be easy, and when it is easy he will like it.

In the mechanical world we reduce friction with oil. In the spiritual world we reduce friction with love. The way to get rid of mental friction, caused by dread, dislike and resistance toward work, persons or situations, is to apply the lubricant of love. If we love the thing we are doing it becomes easier. If we love our enemies they will become friends. Love oils the machinery of life, makes crooked places straight, rough p laces smooth and difficult problems easy. In love is love reflected

Love grows through expression—the more love we express the more we have. It is the great savior and healer of the world. Where there is love there is no deed, no sickness and no unhappiness. Where there is lack of love there is loss and waste. Without love we are without God and without power. We waste our energy, scatter our forces and weaken our lives. With love we are rich, power and complete.

Just as the stingy use of oil in the automobile is poor economy, so stinginess with our love is poor economy. If we withhold our love from someone because they seem unworthy, — then we short-circuit our own good. There is no waste in love, because it benefits the giver and receiver. If the one to whom we direct our love refuses it, then it returns to us.

V
Minimize Your Problems

The first prerequisite of living a happy successful and well-balanced life is to be in absolute harmony with everybody and everything at all times. This, of course, will mean letting others have their own way for the time being, or until your own sense of harmony has so grown that they will willingly follow and cooperate with you. It also will mean an utter disregard of the appearances in your life and in the lives of others. It will mean an expansion of faith in the good a dropping away of the belief in evil.

When Jesus said "Jesus not according to appearances, but judge righteous judgment," He meant that we were to take our attention (conscious thinking) off what "seems to be," and to place it upon what "actually is" the Truth. One is expanding evil and the other is expanding good. One is seeing with the outer eye, the other is beholding the finished Kingdom. One is siding with evil, the other is stripping evil of its power.

Since it is a law of mind that we give life and momentum to which we think about, then we shall arrest the progress of evil by giving is as small room as possible in our thought. In other words, we shall take away the substance that brought it into existence and has been holding it in thought.

When symptoms of evil situations appear, instead of nourishing them by thinking about them and reacting emotionally to them, we need to assume toward them an attitude of Divine indifference, and to turn our attention toward God. We then shall look upon each evil pattern as a mere trifle that soon will disappear. We shall say to each one as it comes: "This, too, shall pass away." Then we shall dismiss the evil from our minds and keep dismissing it until it has spent its power.

"In many instances," says Christian D. Larson, "disease is the result of inharmonious conditions in the body, and all that is necessary to remove both disease and its cause, is to restore harmony. It can truthfully be said that fully twenty percent of the ordinary ailments of life would entirely disappear if perfect harmony were restored to mind and body. Realizing this, we must not permit ourselves to develop any fear of discord. The fear of discord is worse than the discord itself. We should therefore ignore all those conditions completely."

We should ignore those conditions not only because they produce weakness in mind and body, but because they bring many and serious ills. We should train ourselves by expanding our consciousness of God to be bigger than our symptoms and stronger than appearances. How shall we do that? By withholding our thought from evil (meeting it without feeling) and by giving it to God. "Look unto me, and be ye saved, all the ends of the earth." By looking away from evil (meeting I of no import in our thought), and looking unto God, we contract (disintegrate) the pattern of evil and enlarge (magnify) the power of good.

"What is that to thee?" Have you ever really answered that question? "What is that to thee?" What is that symptom or evil situation that has been troubling you? Are you going to make something out of it? Does it mean something to you? Are you storing up energy in it with your thought? Are you giving it momentum through your fear? Are you making it so big through your attention that it is filling your whole consciousness? If so then it is your problem and you Will have to work it out yourself. "What is that to thee?" "Follow thou me."

Haven't you learned that an evil condition can function only so long as its energy lasts, and that when attention is taken away from it the energy has been cut off and the evil weakens and dies. Where is your God at such times? He is right there awaiting your recognition. "If you make your bed in hell I am there." He says, in effect: "I am wherever you are and wherever your evil seems to be. I am in everything and am everywhere at the same time."

Where does the caterpillar go when it leaves the chrysalis? It does not go anywhere. It is absorbed in the butterfly. Where does evil go when you "Judge righteous Judgment?" It does not go anywhere. It is absorbed in the good.

When St. Paul said "None of these things move me" he immediately withdrew from the place of the seeming into the place of Reality; from that which "seems to be" to that "which is." "Judging righteous Judgment" is not praying a certain way,. thinking a certain way or breathing a certain way, but it is the total destruction of that which "seems to be." It is lifting the thoughts to God and being unmoved by the things that appear.

Then the appearances, no matter how terrible they may be, are terminated — the last vestige of power has been taken from them and they begin to weaken, wither and die. The feeling is gone. The air is out of the balloon. The thought structure that kept them in place has collapsed. The unexpected has happened. The evil has disappeared.

Where a man' s consciousness goes, everything else automatically goes with it. His estate goes into court and is soon divided. His body disintegrates. His worldly possessions soon are scattered to the four corners of the earth. Why? Because there is no longer anything to hold them together. When the consciousness is gone then everything else has gone with it. That is why we say that "life is a state of consciousness." It is the state of a man's being and his power of possession. It is everything he has is or hopes to be. It is that which holds him together and enables him to function as a unit.

It would, therefore, be folly to try to remove evil conditions in a man's body or affairs so long as he holds the mental equivalents of those conditions in his consciousness. The drunkard, for instance, may be changed temporarily, but until his consciousness has been changed he will be subject to the same old appetite at any time. When the consciousness is changed, however, the appetite will change with it. Both the desire for liquor and the capacity to become intoxicated will have disappeared.

"Behold, I (Christ Consciousness) make all things new." To get away from evil manifestations, false appetites, inhibitions and the like we must have a new state of consciousness. We must have a new relationship to God." Ye must be born again." :: md things are passed away: behold, all things are become new."

Jesus made it clear that evil conditions could not be changed from the outside. "Of mine ownself," He said, "I can do nothing. The Father within, He doeth the works." He did not counsel men to change the effects but to change the cause — to judge righteous judgment. Knowing that as long as the belief of a particular ailment remained the body would continue to express (outpicture) it He also knew that any effort to change the outer condition was a waste of time.

It is the new that makes life thrilling and interesting and to get the new we must have Christ. We must get rid of old limitations and old beliefs. We must think larger thoughts and see larger vistas. We must expand our consciousness and put the mind in touch with all existence. To get rid of present limitations we must set the mind free. "You have dwelt long enough in this mountain."

Our world is in a constant state of flux and change. Nothing stands still but man's thought and belief. No sooner do women adopt one style of hat and dress than they have to throw them away for others. Ox carts and prairie schooners give way to horses and buggies. Horses and buggies give way to automobiles and airplanes. Candles are changed for kerosene lamps and kerosene lamps are exchanged for electric lights. Old homes are exchanged for new ones. Old books are discarded for better ones.

To live in a world like ours means change, and the faster we change the more alive we become. Life is perpendicular and those who do not climb are thrown into the discard. We must sink or swim. It is change or perish. Life calls and we must answer. "Come over into Macedonia, and help us." "Put your feet into the water and go forward." Leave the place where you are, strike your tents and seek new heights. "Ye have dwelt long enough in this mountain."

The most difficult people to heal are those who refuse to change. That is why Jesus tells us that He has not come to bring peace but a sword. It takes a sword oft times to jar some people out of their negativeness, their passivity and self content. They want something better but they are unwilling to change themselves to get it. "Awake thou that sleepest, arise from the dead, and Christ shall give thee light."

There is a disease born of stagnation and self-complacency which is called arrested development. Those who have this disease are the people who have stopped growing, stopped climbing, stopped making progress. They are only as well as they think they can be and they do not try to become better. They are only as successful as they think they can be and they do not try to improve. They think they are as wise as they can be and do not try to grow wiser. They think they are as high up the hill as they can go and they do not try to climb higher. These people do not respond to ordinary treatment, so God brings a sword to stab them into awareness of their higher possibilities, that He may give them what they need.

One of the most striking and beautiful stories in the Old Testament is the one which compares God's watchfulness over his people to the mother eagle's care for its young. "For the Lord's portion is His people: Jacob is the log of His inheritance. He found him in a desert land, and in the waste howling wilderness; he led him about. He instructed him. He kept him as the apple of His eye. As an eagle stirreth up her nest, fluttereth over her young, spreadeth abroad her wings, taketh them, beareth them on her wings: so the Lord alone did lead him, and there was no strange god with him."

But why does the mother eagle stir up the nest? Why does she expose their tender bodies to the thorns? Why does she push out of their comfortable home to destroy them on the jagged rocks below? Not at all. Eaglets were not made for stagnation in a downy nest of ease. They were made for flight. They were made for the heavens and for the stratosphere. And that is the reason St. Paul tells us to "Stir up the gifts that is within us," and that is why he said "seek those things which are above." We, too, were made for the higher realms and we live but half lives until we find them.

Then, what will you do when the Lord awakens you? Will you rub your eyes and go back to sleep, or will you be about the Father's Business. Will you take forty winks more or will you take your place in Heaven? God has put this book into the hands to wake you up; to awaken you to the realization of your highest possibilities, and to help you get what you need. It is like an alarm clock, however. It will wake you up but it cannot get you out of bed. Whether it succeeds or rails will depend entirely upon you—whether you get up or go back to sleep.

When Isaiah said "Arise, shine; for thy light has come, and the glory of the Lord is risen upon them, "he was telling us that that was as far as God could go. The getting up depends upon us; upon our willingness to follow Him and to make our lives like His Life.

The trouble with most inactive souls is their failure to realize that they were brought into this world to fill a definite place. They feel an inner urge to move upward and forward but they fail to obey it. They become restless or apathetic. While they have an inborn feeling that they could do what they want to do and obtain anything they desire, they do not let themselves go. They have the inner conviction that they could have greater blessings and richer possessions, but they lack the determination and faith that would move them toward the objects they seek.

It is easier to burn candles, say prayers, read psalms, sing hymns, and chant creeds, with no attempt to relate religion to life, or faith to works.

Freedom is not a matter of worship but of conduct. Religion is not a matter of form but of force. If we do not know the Truth then it cannot set us free. If we do not get us to God then God cannot get down to us. We emphasize worship more than conduct, study more than practice, because it is less difficult. Our prayers are hollow, meaningless, tinkling cymbals, because we lack power — because they have no roots. Our desires are unfulfilled because we have made no contact to God. Our days are full of trouble because we are willing to live unmastered lives. We want liberty without law, without a master, and we end up in a "far country."

The philosopher says "express yourself," but never raise the question as to whether we have a self worth expressing. The laws that guide man like the laws that guide the stars are immutable, eternal, and changeless. The Decalogue and the arithmetic table will never be improved. Disregard these laws and they will break you; conform them and they will make you. An unmastered life like an unmastered ship will end in disaster. Being free to do what it wants to do, it is free to do nothing. It never reaches port.

Just as there are natural laws which govern the material world, so there are mental and spiritual laws that govern the conduct of man, endowed with self-choice and free will. The Bible is a text book on the science of living and thinking, just as we have text books on aeronautics, algebra and chemistry. Text books do not represent the final word in science but only the sum total of the information known in a given field. The Romans were masters in civil law; the Greeks in philosophical and aesthetic law, and the Hebrews in codifying moral and spiritual laws. We find the laws of the Hebrews summed up in the twentieth chapter of Exodus (The Ten Commandments), give to Moses by God in Mt. Sinai.

Now let us consider those Ten Commandments in the light of modern psychology and metaphysics and see what they mean to us.

"I am the Lord thy God; thou shalt have none other gods but me." This law sets forth the priority of God. God is the one and only Presence and Power in our lives, and to give power to any but Him is to Cut yourself off from His Good. He is the Absolute, Unconditional Power, which is nothing can limit. "Principle (God) is the absolute, and insofar as any individual can actually induce, within consciousness, upon Principle, a definite concrete acceptance of his desire, it will manifest, even if every thought on earth had to change to compel it."

Everything begins with God as Fist Cause and everything ends with God. He is Alpha and Omega — the beginning and the end. He is the answer to every problem and the fulfillment of every need. This commandment means, then, that we shall put Him first in all our thoughts, desires, prayers, calculations and plans, and that we shall remove from our consciousness all obstructions and hindrances to the inflow of Divine plenty into our lives. We shall do this by refusing to talk, think or read about things that are negative or destructive.

Jesus said, "I and the Father are one." When we harmonize our minds with His Mind, then we can re-enact the Divine Nature — we stop being John Doe and become one with Christ. We re-enact the Divine Nature by holding to and embodying within ourselves only the good, by knowing and accepting nothing but the Presence and Power of God in every person, place, situation and thing.

"Thou shalt not make to thyself any graven thing. . . . Thou shalt not bow down to them, nor worship them." This commandment is a sort of extension of the first one. IT means simply that God can have no rivals and that He will not tolerate divided loyalties. The idols mentioned refer, of course, to anything material or human which may hold the center of our consciousness or affection. These may be friends, loved ones, children, material possessions, riches, problems or difficulties. It has to do with anything on earth which we may give supreme place in our minds or hearts, or to which we may ascribe power. Since God is First Cause, we cannot put anything less than Him first.

It also means that we cannot look to outside sources or agencies for help, guidance or salvation. We must keep our minds open to Him, and close to all else. "God is the goodness of the good." When we trust Him absolutely and allow nothing but Him to have power over us, then we shall prove the Divine Sufficiency in all things.

"Thou shalt not take the name of the Lord thy God in vain." The third Commandment forbids cursing, jokes about sacred things, irreverence and all negative and destructive attitudes towards life. It is the law of reverence and it concerns the sanctity of the name of God. The word name means nature, and to the old Hebrews the name of a person indicated the nature of a person. Thus to curse the name of God was to curse God Himself.

Jesus said: "To this end was I born, and for this cause came I into the world, that I should bear witness unto the Truth.:" If God called His creation good then man is forbidden to call it bad. No matter what it may seem to be on the surface, we must see it, think of it, and speak of it as it is – good. Since God is spirit and man is made in His image and likeness, then man must think of himself (and others) as he is in God, as a spiritual being. He must hold the spiritual (positive) attitude toward life at all times. It is not enough to say that we are sons of God; we also must recognize ourselves to e one with Him.

To keep this commandment, then, we must shut ourselves off from all negation and speak only good of everybody and everything. To live in harmony with Spiritual Law, we must speak the absolute truth and never give expressions to anything else.

"Remember that thou keep holy the Sabbath day." God has set aside one day a week for inspiration, relaxation and rest, and commands us to keep it holy. This means that we must not do any unnecessary work, buy or sell or stay away from church, nor turn Sunday into a day of worldly pleasure. Just as we feed and recharge the physical man six days a week so the spiritual man, if he is to grow, must be fed on Sunday. The sanctity of God's Day is vital to health and all successful living. It cannot be desecrated without serious consequences.

It is an absolute necessity that we have one full day a week in which to renew ourselves in truth and to restore the damage done by the wear and tear of the other six. Dwight L. Moody once said, "If you give up the Sabbath, the church goes; if you give up church, the home goes; and if the home goes the nation goes. That is the direction in which we are traveling."

It is important, therefore, that we set aside one day each week for communion with God and relaxation from all cares, worries, inhibitions and fears, and from all unnecessary tasks. It is one way in which we give God an opportunity to straighten out our difficulties and to work in our behalf. To keep the Sabbath day holy, we must "seek to know, to rest in the Universal rhythm that controls all motion, prevents stagnation, and adds grace and beauty to all that God has created. Enter into the harmony of living and you will decrease the wear and tear upon your body cells."

"Relaxation of the personality is really an evidence of faith and trust. . . . The man who believes absolutely in God, in the divine reliability and goodness, does not hold himself mentally and spiritually rigid, fearful that any moment something is going to happen to him, but, on the contrary, rests in complete confidence that tall things work together for good to them who believe in God. As a result, he has peace in his mind quietness at the center of his life . . .

"This relaxed and peaceful state of mind give him a clear brain, makes possible the clear exercise of all his faculties, and thus he is able to attack his problems with every ounce of ability he possesses. The relaxed man is the powerful man. The rigid, tied-up personality is defeated before the battle starts." (Faith Is The Answer; Blanton and Peale.)

"Honor thy father and thy mother." The fifth commandment relates to the sanctity of the family. The honor called for here refers not alone to parents and those in authority over us, but obedience to God our Father and to the Church our Mother. Someone has said that the most difficult place in the world to be a Christian is in the home. If that is true, then the answer to such a problem is to be found in a more adequate, corporate, religious life; more consideration for one another, more cooperation, a more devotional life, more respect for parents, move love and more understanding. Where there is little respect for parents, there is little respect for God.

Jesus called us "friends." What a tribute! If parents and children, brothers and sisters could be friends as well as relatives, it would not only strengthen and spiritualize the home but nation as well. Interpreted metaphysically, this commandment means that we must accept the love of God and take our place in the divine plan as the "Son," or perfect expression of Divine Love, and that we be obedient to the law of love at all times, in all places and under all circumstances.

The parable of the Prodigal Son is in reality an illustration of the relationship between the individual and his parent, God. However far a man way wander or separate himself from true goodness, the way back always is through obedience or conformity to the law of love. When we turn from absorption in self and center ourselves in God, we are restored as honored guests in the Father's House.

"Thou shalt do no murder." This commandment has to do with sanctity and forbids anger in every form, thought, word and deed. To murder means to kill, to cut off, to separate from life. Jesus said: "It is written that thou shalt not kill, but I say unto you, that whosoever is angry with his brother hath committed murder in his heart already." In this statement Jesus again is taking man back to the source of all his trouble—his thinking. If there were no murderous thoughts there would be no murder. If there were no angry thoughts there would be no fatal blows.

To realize the importance of this announcement as touching human conduct we need only recount the crimes of anger that fill our prisons, the good positions lost because of temper, careers crippled by uncontrolled passion; the grief that has been cause by violent quarrels, families broken up by storms of rage, nerves shattered by temporary madness, hearts weakened by fretting, scolding and fuming—the terrible havoc that has been created by malevolence, bitterness and hatred.

It is a well known fact that a violent fit of temper or anger many times not only reverse the mental and physical processes of the mind and body, stop the action of the heart and produces apoplexy, but will wrench and rack the delicate nervous system and vitiate the blood as no other passion can do. It is temporary insanity, or an emotional tornado, which does more permanent damage and more irreparable injury to the entire mental and physical being than any other one thing.

The antidote for anger is love, peace, and self-control. Shakespeare says, "Assume a virtue if you have it not," and Emerson, in effect, says: "Assume as already yours the virtue you would like to have; appropriate it; enter into the part, live the character just as does the great actor absorbed in the character he plays." Regardless of how great your capacity for anger and bad temper may be, refuse to express it. Instead assume the virtue of love. When tempted to "fly to pieces" over some provocative act, just assume the calm, quiet, deliberate, balanced composure which characterizes a son of God, and repeat to yourself the words: "God in me maintains the harmony of my being."

"Thou shalt not commit adultery." To most people the seventh commandment refers only to the sacredness of sex and to the marriage of divorced persons, if the other still is living, etc., etc., but it means much more than that. It also forbids impurity in every form (particularly in thought) immodesty, immoderation, excesses, overeating, drinking, and laziness.

Adultery peculiarly is the sin of the adult. An adulterer is anybody who sees double and make things appear different than they are. He loses the original state of a thing by making something else out of it. The adult is double-minded while the child is single-minded. The adult sees both good and evil; the child sees only the good. The child sees and accepts the truth while the adult, believe in two powers and two presences, adulterates his consciousness of the Truth. He sees and hears the Truth but to him it doesn't seem to be Truth. The Truth is there but he does not recognize it because of his double-mindedness.

We have pure-food laws today which say, "Thou shalt not commit adultery," because adulteration immediately creates something else than that intended by law — another substance. The original is lost, submerged, as when the man puts sand in his sugar. It no longer is sugar though there still is a sugar content. In order to restore the sugar to its original state it would need to be purified by removing, sifting out the sand. And so it is with our minds.

To keep this commandment, then, we must be obedient not alone to the laws of sex and marriage, but we also must cleanse our minds of all impure thoughts and of all place where we know that God is the only Presence and Power in our lives, and where there is none else beside Him. Jesus said, "Blessed are the pure in heart: for they shall see God." The pure in heart are those whose vision is one-pointed. They are those who know God to the exclusion of all else, who live in His Presence here and now, without any mixture of belief in His absence.

"It is written," said Jesus "that thou shalt not commit adultery, but I say unto you, that whosoever looketh on a woman to lust after her hath committed the act already." If there were no adulterous thoughts there would be no adultery.

"Thou shalt not steal." When one hears this commandment read he usually dismisses it with the thought that it does not apply to him. He thinks of it more as a law governing habital thieves and those who steal from others. It means that, of course but much more. In the church we speak of this commandment as the law of sacredness of property, but it also forbids gambling, cheating, copying — dishonesty of every kind; and it includes withholding our money from God, and acquiring physical and material blessings by other means than by right of consciousness.

"Through wisdom is an house builded; and by understanding it is established: And by knowledge shall the chambers be filled with all precious and pleasant riches." Since the basis of all attraction and permanence of possessions is in consciousness, then anything that is acquired by any other means, whether it be health, money or property, will be only temporary. It will remain with us only until some superior force takes it away. There is a just compensation for every possession and without the compensation the possession cannot last.

The Source of our supply is inscribed on our American money — "In God we trust." But we trust the money rather than the Source. We forget the Source and so live in uncertainty and fear. We withhold from Him Who provides, and so shut off our supply. We shut it off by taking from God what rightfully is His. We break our contact with Creative Power by withholding the title.

"The law of tithing is the law of sowing and reaping. Where there is a definite contact preserved between cause and effect, the effect is supported and perpetuated. If a break in the process occurs, the effect must diminish accordingly. When the Prodigal Son separated his inheritance from the Father it soon dissipated itself. The law is to perpetuate and amplify whatever it is allowed to act upon. Tithing preserves this contact," and withholding breaks it. Let us, therefore, keep this contact "by returning to God that which belongs to Him as the Source of all" that we are and have.

"Thou shalt not bear false witness." The ninth law deals with the sacredness of our word, and commands truthfulness. It also forbids lies about ourselves and others, gossip, false excuses and every kind of pretense. "Ye shall know the Truth, and the Truth shall make you free." God knows the Truth, but before we can build our lives and affairs around it, we ourselves must know it.

Even though everything seems to be against us, we must be able to say from the center of our consciousness: "These things do not matter a whit, for they are not true of God. God will shine through them and dissolve them as sunlight dissolves shadows. God is in charge in His Realm of Spirit, and nothing can stand against Him. My trust is in God. He will tell me in plenty of time what I of my human self should do."

The trouble with most people when they pray is, that they give more attention to their needs and their limitations than to God, and this is bearing false witness. They want God to set them free in the outer world without first setting them free in the inner world and this cannot be done. "Seek ye first the Kingdom of God." The inner (spiritual world) comes first, because it is there that we receive power to rule the outer.

In an article "Remaking Our World," Imelda Octavia Shanklin says: "The power by which we act upon the Spiritual Creation is the same power by which Creation came. The power is the word . . . The Spiritual Creation never changes, being the form of God's immutable word. Our world continually is changing, being made in the form of our fickle words.

"Our world is constituted of all that we hold in consciousness, and words react upon consciousness . . . When we speak a new word, our world is changed somewhat. If we reiterate the new word, the change is strengthened. A new word may have the power radically to change our world, to change it constantly. But the making of our world rarely is instantaneous. Our mind swings from the good that we hope to manifest and again contemplates the non-good which we hope to expel from our midst . . . The measure of our belief is indicated by the effect of the re-creating word. 'God said . . . and it was so."

Do you now see the importance of this commandment? It means that we dare not give power to distressing conditions in the outer world when we are trying to get a right, subjective recognition in the inner world. God cannot forgive us if we believe more in the power of evil than in the power of good. Neither can He relieve our distresses if we believe more in them than we do in Him, if we keep our minds filled with our troubles.

"Thou shalt not covet." We break the tenth commandment by being discontented and selfish, in magnifying our misfortunes rather than our blessings, and by being envious and covetous of what others have. Contentment is not a state of having but of being. It has nothing to do with one's physical possessions, nor the lack of them. It comes to rich and poor alike, and grows out of an harmonious and balanced state of mind.

The contented person neither envies nor covets; he appreciates what he himself possesses and seeks to better his condition— he does not find fault with things as they are, but promotes improvement. Knowing that better things are on the way, he acknowledges the good he already has and enjoys it. He is contented with the present but builds more lofty mountains for the future. The covetous, on the other hand, is a lazy person—he has not taken possession of his own, and he does not get more because he is not grateful for what he has. Without gratitude, he cannot contact his Source.

The most pressing problem in practical religion is that of getting people to stand upon their own centers, to be self-reliant, self-maintained, self-governed; to raise their minds to a new level of consciousness and to get them to trust that consciousness for everything they need. Since we all are heirs to the same Power and the same Mind which was also in Christ Jesus, there is no reason why we ever should envy or covet, or look to others for our good.

In God-consciousness we not only are the masters of our destinies, but we have the power to transform ourselves and our world, and to get anything we need. St. Pau said, "Be ye transformed by the renewing of your mind." As we relate ourselves constructively to the Creative Power, we shall attract the good things in abundance.

Jesus said, "Think not that I am come to destroy the law, or the prophets: I am not come to destroy, but to fulfill." All Divine laws can be fulfilled in our lives by strict obedience to them. They were given for our benefit and not for our restriction. It is impossible to break the laws of God, but we can break ourselves by trying to live outside them. It is Christ or chaos for every man. It is liberty under law or bondage outside law; and every man must choose which course he will take.

VI
Laws

Now let us note briefly some of the laws which Jesus gave for the benefit of mankind.

THE LAW OF HUMILITY

"Whosoever shall exalt himself shall be abased; and he that shall humble himself shall be exalted." In metaphysics we refer to this law as the law of "reverse effort," which means simply that we receive the exact opposite of what we ask when our relation to the law is wrong. If we are related to the law negatively, then regardless of what we ask the results will be negative. If we are related to the law positively, then the results will be positive.

Jesus "believed that if you keep yourself out of the picture others will put you in the picture if you should be there." If you keep yourself out of your consciousness, then God will fill it with His Presence.

The reason humility is so important in spiritual work is because it opens the valve toward God, so that His blessings can flow in. The meek man is like a magnet, drawing everything and everybody to himself. Having emptied himself of himself, he is open to God. The profound or self sufficient, on the other hand, is just the opposite of the meek. He does not attract people and blessings, but repels them. Being so full of his own opinions and egotism, he has no room for anything else. He crowds out the better things by his preoccupation with the lesser.

THE LAW OF RETRIBUTION

"With what judgment ye judge, ye shall be judged; and with what measure ye mete, it shall be measured to you again." This law means that what we give out comes back to us. When we are generous we receive generously in return. When we are kind others are kind to us. When we are fearful we attract trouble. When we are ugly we bring out ugliness from others. "When we are critical, we draw criticism from others."

Now read this text again and you will see that it is Jesus' way of telling you that your happiness and achievement depends not upon people, circumstances or situations, but upon yourself. Your life is in your own hands to do with it as you please. It will be what you make it. It will give back to you exactly what you put into it—no more, no less.

But let us analyze this law from the other end. Let us suppose that you are the recipient instead of the sender of some injustice. Let us suppose that someone has wilfully injured you, what are you to do? The answer is, nothing. "Vengeance is mine—I will repay," saith the Lord. This is the law of the boomerang; the law of action and reaction. It is nature's way of fighting our battles for us. Just as a rubber ball will return to us with the same force with which it is thrown against the wall, so the evil sent out by us will return to us. It will return in spite of anything we can do to stop it. The judgment precedes the act, thus relieving you of all retaliation and "getting even."

THE LAW OF SACRIFICE

"He that findeth his life shall losse it: and he that loseth his life for my sake shall find it." A man's consciousness is like a stream of flowing water. If the stream is dammed by self, the water settles in all the low places and becomes sour and inactive. The quickest way to purify and reclaim the low places in consciousness is not only to let in the Christ from above but to open the dam (remove the self) below. Many people try to demonstrate God in their affairs by repeating affirmations of Truth, but they fail to let go of self and the blessings cannot get through.

To surrender self, on the other hand, creates a spiritual vacuum that draws more blessings to fill the vacant places. Rich living is but the return circuit of a detached self. What we give away we keep, whether it be self, money or anything else. Give and it shall be given unto you. Withhold and you shall lose.

The self-centered consciousness is like a magnet for evil. It not only will draw disease and much sickness into its life, and trouble into its surroundings, but eventually will go to pieces spiritually, mentally and physically. Shutting itself up within itself, it closes itself off from God and from others. Dr. Fritz Kunkel says: "It has been shown that all mistakes, weaknesses and aberrations can be traced back to man's ego-centricity. According, the fundamental problem of self-education may be described as the problem of overcoming one's own ego-centricity." (God Helps Those . . . p. 135.)

How then shall we overcome self-centeredness? There is only one way. We must die to the self. We must die to the lesser self that the greater self may live. St. Paul said, "For me to die is gain"; and, again, "Put off the old man and put on the new man, which is Christ." What did he mean? What did Jesus mean by losing the life to find it? He meant that we were to free ourselves mentally from the idea that we are separate from God. Dying to self does not mean freeing ourselves from the individuality, or body, but freeing ourselves from the idea of ourselves as separate from God.

It is the idea (belief) in separation that is to die (become inactive), and not the individual. "Where the Spirit of the Lord is, there is liberty." We are free from the personal self when we are convinced that we are not separate from God but one with Him. When we are free from the delusion of separation, then we are free from all the ills of the flesh.

THE LAW OF PROVISION

"Seek ye first His Kingdom and His righteousness; and all these things shall be added unto you." This means to expand your consciousness in every direction until it includes everything good. Expand it to include your body, your affairs and everybody in your world. "Seek ye first His Kingdom" means to increase your capacity for God. Center yourself in the consciousness of His Presence. Look to Him, trust Him, have faith in Him as the Source of all your good. Let His Spirit guide you in all that you do and say: and everything you need will come to you. You will become a magnet for everything good because you have related your self constructively to your Source.

God is everywhere evenly present. Realize this and He will fill every part of your world with His Perfection. Let His consciousness fill your body and all sickness will vanish before it. Let it fill your mind and all trouble will disappear from your world. Let Him have full charge of your consciousness and He will arrange everything for the best, for your highest good.

The entrance to the Kingdom of God is not through the portals of death, but through the gates of consciousness — wisdom and understanding. You enter it, not by going somewhere physically, but by changing your mind and expanding your consciousness. The Kingdom of God is not on Pike's Peak, in New York or in New Jersey. It is in your own heart and mind. You are in It when you realize God's Presence, and out of It when you think only of self and all the problems and difficulties attached thereto.

You may be in the Kingdom or outside It, it all depends upon your mental attitude toward life. If your attitude is harmonious, then, regardless of where you are or what you are doing, you are in the Kingdom of God. If your attitude is inharmonious, then you are outside the Kingdom.

It is clear therefore that this law has to do with the increase of one's capacity. Since God will fill any measure we hold up to Him, then the way to get more is to increase the size of the measure. This is not done by cramming the Kingdom of God into a small mind, but by expanding the mind. It is done by taking the largest possible view of everything, by living in tune with the Limitless and by harmonizing our thought with God's thought. When the outer man declares that you cannot do a certain thing, then respond by saying, "The Kingdom of God is within me, therefore I can do anything I need to do."

THE LAW OF CHOICE

"Ye cannot serve God and mammon." Jesus' statement in the parable that "a certain man had two sons" points out the possibility of experiencing both good and evil. Moses revealed the same thing when he told the children of Israel that he had set before them a blessing and a curse, and that they must choose whom they would serve. Just as there are two ways of looking at the things that happen to us, so there are two ways of looking at life. One brings health, happiness and success, while the other brings sickness, misery and failure.

There is just one Power, and the way we relate ourselves to It is what counts. If we relate ourselves to It destructively, then the power will be misdirected. It then will not go where it is supposed to go and evil conditions will be created. If we are related to It constructively, then It will be directed into constructive channels and will create good conditions.

Thus it is evident that they way to overcome evil is by choosing the good, by removing false ideas and "creating true ideas." Evil will then disappear in the exact portion that we cease to believe in it, while good will come to us in the precise degree that we embody it. When we stop the dual act of believing both in the Presence and the absence of God, and turn with our whole being to the One, then evil will be swallowed up in the good. "I will forgive their iniquity, and I will remember their sin no more." That is, our sin will be wiped out completely; it will cease to exist.

Live constantly in the inner conviction that God is the only Presence and Power in your life, never compromising with anything less than the fullness of God; and you soon will discover that something is happening in your life that never happened before. "DO NOT TRY TO MAKE THINGS HAPPEN; SIMPLY KNOW THAT THEY ARE HAPPENING. Daily realize your unity with the Whole and the Unity of the Whole with you. YOU SOON WILL DEVELOP SUCH A POWERFUL PERSONALITY THAT ALL WHO COME IN CONTACT WITH YOU WILL WISH TO REMAIN IN YOUR PRESENCE."

THE LAW OF PRAYER

"Ask and it shall be given unto you; seek, and ye shall find."

"Whatsoever things ye desire, when ye pray, believe that ye receive them, and ye shall have them."

This is God's law of prayer. The Infinite knows our needs before we ask Him; but prayer completes a circuit which opens the mind to receive.

THE STEPS IN PRAYER

I. BALANCE YOUR MIND. Before God can fill our emptiness with His fullness, we must have a consciousness of oneness, order and completeness. To get a larger measure of His good, we must remove everything that would deny that good. We must purify our minds of all that is at variance with His Will. The man who comes to God with a large capacity (receptivity) will receive a large gift; the man who comes with a small measure will receive a small gift. "Since all things are yours," as St. Paul said, then our measure of God's blessings always will be as large as our conscious realization of those blessings.

It does not make any difference how large the measure may be, it will be filled. Do you understand what that means? It means that there is no limit to what God can and will do for you when you have His Mind, and you have His mind when your own mind is divested of all thought of self.

The first step in prayer, then, is to purify the mind, to neutralize all false beliefs, to drop the negations, and to counteract every acid thought. Why is this necessary? Because the cleansing of consciousness puts us in the right psychological and metaphysical position toward God. "Blessed are the pure in heart: for they shall see God." Before a man buys an automobile he makes a place for it by providing a garage. Before a man receives a new blessing from God he must make a place for it in his mind. He must get rid of everything that would in any way contradict, oppose or deny its Presence.

That is why St. James told us to confess our faults. We must remove and erase completely all old mistakes. We must forgive ourselves and everybody. We must forget all problems, troubles, difficulties, worries, fears and injustices. We must let go completely and wipe them out altogether. We must not hold on to anything that would in any way dim the brilliance of that which is to heal and make us whole.

II. RELAX THE MIND. The second step is to relax the mind. Just as the sky cannot be reflected on troubled waters so the Presence of God cannot be felt by a restless soul. "Be still and know that I am God." "In quietness and in confidence shall be your strength." "The Lord is in his holy temple: let all the earth keep silence before Him." "Be silent all flesh before Jehovah." "My soul, wait thou in silence for God only; for my expectation is from Him" When we realize that in quietness and in confidence is the only way we can get to God, and the only way He can get to us, then we shall be meticulous in our obedience to the laws of silence.

The silence always is there waiting for us to enter it. It is the Christ. Center in the midst of our being. It "is the Holy Place of God active at the heart of all creation." When you enter there, you are one with the Power of God. He talks with you and you talk with Him. You listen to Him and He listens to you. Automatically you close the doors of your mind to all wretched, weak thoughts and distressing conditions in the outer world. You drop all negation, limited, puny and destructive thoughts, and fill your mind with God's flawless and undeviating perfection, and make claim to it as your own. You subvert and transcend everything that might contradict your wholeness and perfection in Him.

Silence is another name for Practicing the Presence of god. It is a cooperative endeavor which not only establishes more firmly your contact with God, but brings the best out of the Universe and the best out of you. It brings the inner self to the surface and into the presence of God. It is that condition in which you can speak the word that shall not return unto you void.

III. DECIDE WHAT YOU WANT. Before the thing asked for can be produced in your experience it first must be created in your mind. You must have it as a mental equivalent. All things whatsoever ye ask in prayer must start in the realm of cause (consciousness) before they can become an effect on the material plane. To materialize a desire you must not only ask, believe and have faith, but you need to maintain with confidence your image (hold to it) in the Higher Consciousness. In other words, you must cooperate actively with the thing you have asked for or there will be no successful progress in your prayer. You must know that God is omnipresent in every circumstance, waiting only for your acknowledgment and claim.

IV. ASK FOR WHAT YOU WANT. "Ye shall ask what ye will, and it shall be done unto you." — "If thou canst believe, all things are possible to him that believeth." The act of asking God for some blessing immediately sets into operation the Creative Power which has produced the whole universe. It not only clarifies and defines the object of your desire, but puts it in the best possible position to be acted upon by the Creative Power of God. Coupled with your faith and belief, it will bring into play the whole Force of Divine Mind in fulfilling your desire.

V. GET A CLEAR REALIZATION OF THE BLESSING ASKED FOR. When you make your mental demand, or claim, let the clear realization of the answer form itself in your mind. Stay your mind upon it. Let it occupy a definite place in the center of your consciousness. As St. Paul said, "Let Christ be formed in you." Let the object of your prayer form in you a consciousness of itself. The reason many people receive unwanted things in their experience is because they allow negative images to form in their minds.

VI. UNITE YOUR MIND WITH GOD'S MIND. To get through prayer the things you desire, your mind and God's mind must be united perfectly in one objective. Your conscious and subconscious minds must be synchronized perfectly. This means that the whole force of your being must be in your request or your prayer will fail. You must desire an answer with all your heart, all your mind, all your strength and with all your soul. "Let every soul be subject unto higher powers. For there is no power but of God."

Recognize this truth and then take the next step: "Let this mind be in you, which was also in Christ Jesus: who, being in the form of God, thought it not robbery to be equal with God." The first six words of the Lord's Prayer mean literally: Raise your thoughts to God—raise them to Heavenly places, or places of perfection.

VII. PRAY IN THE WILL OF GOD. Never say, "God thought it best not to give me what I asked," but rather, "I failed to receive what I asked because of my lack of belief and faith." Since prayer is not a game of chance but an exact law, then the only thing that can prevent us from receiving from God is lack of belief and faith—Jesus said we fail because of our ignorance of the correct use of the law. "But who so looketh into the perfect law of liberty and CONTINUETH therein, he being not a forgetful hearer, but a doer of the word, this man shall be blessed in his deed."

It is improper therefore ever to take the attitude that it may not be God's will for you to have a particular thing. God's Will is good will and He has no choice but to give you good. When you fulfill the conditions of Payers, He always gives you what you ask, and experience teaches what is best for you to have. The evil in your life was not brought by God but by you because of your opposition to His Will.

VIII. GET A SENSE OF SELF-MASTERY. Know that when you pray you are dealing with Absoluteness, and that therefore you are equal to every occasion. "With God all things are possible." There is no disease too terrible, no problem too complex and no obstacle too great; there is no difficulty too big that you cannot dissipate it by the power of your word—if your union with God is complete. "I can do all things through Christ which strengtheneth me." In dealing with Truth you are dealing with a force that you cannot fool. God is able, and will do anything you believe that He can do, if you refuse to recognize any concessions or limitations and if you know in your heart that nothing can interfere with your prayer.

IX. WRITE OUT YOUR PRAYER. When a new image has been formed in the mind, there is a distinct advantage in writing it down. This is done to impress it more deeply upon the subconscious self. Committing it to paper helps to seal it in your consciousness — to give it depth. As a seed must be planted in the ground before we can reap a harvest so our prayer must be implanted in the soul (integrated with God) before it can be answered. It must reach a point of acceptance and an unqualified and undisputed place of agreement in consciousness. "Out of the heart (subconscious mind) are the issues of life."

The way to materialize a desire scientifically is to keep the thought changed into the new image. We must take it up in meditation daily and recognize that it already is an accomplished fact in experience. We should accept the idea that the desire already is integrated (embodied) in God. We should involve the image (object of desire) in mind until the Creative Power accepts it as its own and we do that by repetition, and by belief and acceptance.

By putting the object of our desire on paper, we impress it more deeply upon the mind and commit ourselves more fully to its realization. Let us make it final, then, by declaring, "What I have written I have written."

X. THANK GOD FOR THE ANSWER. "With thanksgiving," said St. Paul, let your requests be made known unto God." The best evidence of our belief that we have received what we ask is when we thank God for the blessing before it appears. The prayer of thanksgiving really is praying three ways at the same time. It is the prayer of Recognition (seeing the thing desired in manifestation); Realization (accepting it as already an accomplished fact), and Revelation (the Divine response to our request). It is the practice of the Presence of God.

First, we mentally choose what we want; we mentally lay hold of the good we desire through recognition. We magnify (expand) it through realization, and we release it into expression, revelation, through the acknowledgment of thanksgiving. It now is a part of our consciousness; we attract it by virtue of what we are. That is, we demonstrate our consciousness of it, whereas before we demonstrated our unconsciousness of it.

Contrary to the belief of many otherwise well informed people, we do not demonstrate things but only our consciousness of things. We demonstrate our consciousness at all times and never anything else. We do not set a time at which the demonstration is to be made, for there is no time but now. We do not worry and fret when the answer does not come, but simply lift our hearts to God and thank Him every time the desire appears to our thought. This keeps our mind centered in the One Activity, which is perfect. Nothing has hindered; nothing can short-circuit it: it always is operating, always working in our behalf.

Jesus understood this method of prayer when, before there was any tangible evidence of the answer, He said, "I thank Thee, Father, that Thou hast heard me. And I know that Thou hearest me always." It was not His words alone that caused the power to come into manifestation, but His belief and faith that that which He had asked the Father for already was His. "God, I thank Thee" is the full recognition and realization that the thing is taking place here and now. "He that hath Spirit (inner acceptance) hath the sign also."

"If we know that the Power with which we are dealing is Principle, and not personality; if we know and believe that

Mind (Spirit) is the only Actor, Cause, Effect, Substance, Intelligence, Truth and Power that there is; and if we have a real embodiment of our desires, then we can thank God for the manifestation and be assured of results."

XI. RELEASE THE DESIRE FROM PERSONAL THOUGHT. The last step in scientific prayer is to get the desire out of our hands and into God's Hands. Why? Because "the natural man (conscious mind) receiveth not the things of God": As long as the desire is held tightly in the personal thought it is impossible for God to do anything about it. It must, as Jesus said, be released. It must be dropped out of the conscious mind and be in complete detachment and forgetfulness. "Spiritual things are spiritually discerned."

If the other conditions of answered prayer have been met, "The Spirit must now go forth into Creation through law and action. The see must be dropped into the ground and allowed to rot, and the desire must be freed in the same way. The worry, anxiety, uncertainty and fear must be taken away. The desire must be allowed to push its roots down into the subconscious mind and push itself up again into the conscious mind. It now is out of our hands and we must take no more thought about it." When God takes charge then shall He positively have our answer. Every idea that is planted (integrated) in the subconscious mind will produce an effort exactly like its cause.

These laws were not given for our punishment but for our advancement. If we conform to them, they will bless us. If we disobey them, they will punish us. As individuals with self-choice, we are perfectly free to disobey them, but we are not free to escape the consequences of disobedience. Laws by and of themselves are impersonal and inflexible. They work the way we use them. They relate themselves to us the way we relate ourselves to them. They never make any allowances for mistakes, nor do they ever work contrary to their own nature.

No one ever has broken the laws of God, but many have hurt themselves in trying to do so. The same laws that give to us when we obey them take away from us when we disobey them. Let us therefore conform to the laws which God has ordained, that through them we may be brought again to the Kingdom of Heaven, where all our desires are fulfilled.

The important thing in working with Spiritual Law is the recognition that the good we seek already is in manifestation and that we are, in reality, not demonstrating anything but waking up to that which already is demonstrated. The statement in the parable that "He divided unto them his living" also implies that there was an abundance in the Father's House and that the son recognized it instinctively.

VII
The Answer

ACKNOWLEDGMENT; COOPERATION;
READJUSTMENT

We all feel that if we could get close to God, life would be very different, our needs would be met, our diseases healed and our states of separation be turned into oneness. It is a spiritual certainty inborn in us. We know instinctively that where God is there is no lack, and that to be united with Him is to draw from the Inner Source everything that we need. The son recognized this and as he recognized it, "it automatically operated for him."

It was a Persian philosopher who said, "That which ought to be, is; therefore let us rest." That which ought to be is NOW. That which is, and ought to be, is GOOD. That which is, and ought to be, is perfect. There are not two creations, the one material and the other spiritual. There is only ONE. There are not two powers, the one evil and the other good. There is only — God the Good. What seems to be material, what seems to be evil, is nothing more than a state of consciousness which is out of adjustment with Divine Law. We do not know life as it is and so we get a material reaction to it.

How strange that it should take the followers of Christ nearly two thousand years to discover that the Kingdom of God is not a geographical place, to be attained through suffering and death, but our ideal state of mind, already perfected by Christ and only awaiting our recognition and experience of It. In some ways contemporary religion reminds us of the old mazes of the Seventeenth Century, built in the gardens to confuse trespassers, a confusing network of meandering paths that led nowhere.

Jesus said: "Ye seek me for the loaves and fishes and cannot find me." We build our mazes by trying to demonstrate things instead of demonstrating our consciousness. Use this technique, says one. Breathe this way, says another. Avoid starches, says someone else. Follow the stars. Study the pyramids. Gaze into the crystal! Go to this fortune teller. Study spiritualism. Take this course. Think this way. Go to that church, go to this church, etc., etc.

Now contrast the above with what Jesus says: "No man cometh unto the Father, but by me"; and, again, "Leave all and follow me." Spiritual demonstration is not a question of getting something from the outside, but of realizing something which already is within us—the Kingdom of God. It is working up to, or becoming conscious of that which we already have, and then being that thing.

"What you are," said Emerson, "screams so loud that I cannot hear what you say." What you are is what the world is telling you. What you are is what you are attracting from the world. A man's mind, personality and character do have a way of advertising him to others. He does this in the carriage of the body, the tone of the voice, the expression of the face, and the manner of dress; in gestures, in things he does and says, and in the things he refrains from doing and saying. Man's every movement tells abroad his nature, what he thinks and what he is; for he is what he thinks.

In his essay on "Spiritual Laws," Emerson says: "Human character evermore publishes itself. The most fugitive deed and word, the mere air of doing a thing, the intimated purposes expresses character: if you sit still, if you sleep you show it." As Michelangelo stood gazing at a block of marble, he shouted, "There is an angel in that marble." But he could just as well have seen a devil, and brought it forth. What he saw within the marble was what he had within himself. A man cannot remain apart from that which he is. Therefore that which we wish to have or express we first must be. Hearing and being history is the difference between reading and making it. To have is temporary and transitory; to be is eternal.

In the feeding of the five thousand, as recorded in the Fourteenth chapter of St. Matthew's gospel, the disciples were facing a real problem. They had come to the lake for a rest and a retreat with their Master. They were tired and they wanted to be alone. They wanted Him to themselves. But their plans were frustrated. Their boat had hardly touched the shore when a great multitude of people swooped down upon them. The demands of the multitude were so insistent that they took up all Jesus' time.

The disciples obviously were annoyed and they were out of patience. They had worked hard and the end of the day was not yet in sight. It was now twilight and yet these people do not go away. They have been there all day without food and they are hungry. There are no grocery stores or restaurants in this isolated spot, and if there had been the disciples lacked sufficient money to buy food for them.

Then, to make the situation worse, Jesus is not doing anything about it. He is so preoccupied with His teaching and healing that he seemingly has forgotten all about food and time. The disciples love Him devotedly. But they think He is a bit impractical. They do not yet trust Him as they should. They feel He needs to be taken in hand, and told what to do. It is now evening and He keeps on with His ministrations. Will He never stop? Doesn't He know where He is? Doesn't He know the time of day? Isn't He hungry Himself.

There is one thing only for the disciples to do — they must take the situation into their own hands and do with it the best they can.

What a familiar ring this story has in our modern life. It belongs not only to Jesus' day and time but to ours also. Life constantly is bringing us problems and difficulties to which there seems to be no solution. "Again and again we come to veils through which we cannot see and doors to which we find no key. Over and over we are met by demands for which our resources seem inadequate."

We are like the disciples. We follow religion but it does nothing for us. Our consciousness of God is smaller than our needs, and so we accept the burdens as our own. We either muddle through them in our own strength or get out from under.

Instead of making our consciousness bigger than our needs, we "pass the buck" to someone else. "Send the multitude away," the disciples urged. There was nothing they could do about feeding so many hungry people, so they would shift the responsibility.

How familiar that is, too, and how applicable to our time. The Bible is full of such instances, and so is modern life. When Jeremiah was sent to a congregation which tried him to the limit, his only thought was how to escape. Listen to him: "I wish I had a lodging place in the wilderness for wayfaring men; that I might leave my people, and go from them." And look at Jonah when he was sent up to Ninevah. "Jonah rose up to flee into Tarshish from the presence of the Lord."

We lament such behavior in prophets and preachers, but we forget that we all have done the same thing ourselves. When others disagree with us, we cut them off. When partners fail to get along, the partnership is dissolved. When friends fall out, the friendship is broken. When domestic difficulties arise, we run to the divorce court. When things do not suit us in one church, we run to another. When trouble multiplies too fast, we try only to dodge it. We always are running away from something or somebody.

"But Jesus said unto them. They need not depart; give ye them to eat." The disciples did not dodge the issue because they were callous or indifferent to the hunger of the crowd, but because they felt unable and inadequate to meet the need. Having taken an inventory of their assets, they found that they had but five loaves and two fishes. Just imagine, only five loaves and two little fish for five thousand people. Why it is not enough to give each one a small crumb.

Is that all you have? Are you sure you have no other resources? Are you sure that that is all you can get? "That is all," they answer with a tone of finality.

Then why don't you consult your Master? Why don't put put the problem up to Him? Has He ever refused your requests? Has He ever failed to give you what you asked? Is it not possible that He has a solution to this problem and that if you would stop magnifying your poverty and look to Him He would give it to you? Why do you leave Him out of the picture? Has it occurred to you that you do not need to meet this difficult situation alone, and that "My God shall supply all your needs according to His riches in glory by Christ Jesus."

No, it hadn't occurred to them because they thought of Jesus as being so idealistic and preoccupied with other things that He did not even recognize the need. They did not know that He already had sensed the emergency, and, as St. John says, "knew what He would do." The disciples had a plan and Jesus had a plan. The disciples, seeing only their poverty, reacted to the situation negatively. They would send the people away to shift for themselves.

Jesus, seeing only the omnipresence of God, reacted positively. He would keep the multitude there. He would take a bad situation and turn it into a good one. He would prove that God had an answer for every problem and a supply for every need. The disciples, looking at their five loaves and two fishes, saw only limitation and inadequacy, while Jesus saw abundance and plenty.

"And they say unto Him, We have here but five loaves, and two fishes. He said, Bring them hither to me. And He commanded the multitude to sit down on the grass (put themselves in a receptive position), and took the five loaves, and the two fishes, and looking up to heaven, he blessed, and brake, and gave the loaves to his disciples, and the disciples to the multitude. And they did all eat, and were filled: and they took up of the fragments that remained twelve baskets full. And they that had eaten were about five thousand men, besides women and children."

This story really is a lesson in cooperation — the union of man-power and God-Power. The miracle was accomplished not by

Jesus alone, nor by the disciples alone, but by Jesus and the disciples working together with God. That is how all human needs are met and how all great demonstrations are made. St. Paul, telling of the stupendous growth of the Christian religion in Rome, said: "I have planted, Apollus watered; but God gave the increase," and that is the meaning of "Thy Kingdom come on earth as it is in heaven."

The Kingdom of God is to come, and new conditions are to be made, not by man alone, nor by God alone, but by man and God working together.

The story is told of a retired miner who had settled on a plot of ground at the edge of a small city in Montana. The spot had been desolate but, thanks to his hard work and care, it had become a garden spot. The local minister called and praised the beauty of the place. The old man was not much given to church going and the minister wanted to impress him with the importance of God's help. "Well, John, you and God certainly have made this place beautiful." To which the old fellow, after pondering, finally replied: "Yes, I guess so; but you should have seen it when only God had it."

This is an apt description of our situation many times today. We either leave it all to God or leave Him out of the picture altogether. We seek spiritual benefits but we do not change our consciousness in order to get them; we do not keep our minds open to receive them. We study and listen but we do nothing about what we read and hear. St. James said: "Be ye doers of the word, and not hearers only, deceiving your own selves." There is no question but that God will give the increase, but we must sow the seed and cultivate it. "Apart from me ye can do nothing."

God is dependent upon us and we are dependent upon God. To build a new world for us, He not only needs our minds to think through, but our lips to speak with, our hands to work with and our feet to walk with. We should not do as the disciples did, spend our time bewailing our material liabilities, but we should take account of our Spiritual assets.

It makes no difference what the problem or need, if the subconscious mind recognizes that God is everywhere evenly present, that "Heaven and earth are full of Thee," then the problem will be solved and the need supplied quickly. That is the modus operandi of all Spiritual achievement. "God is everywhere evenly present." "I am here, there and everywhere." Repeat these statements every time you sense any lack in your body or affairs. Get the feeling of plenty and abundance everywhere. Let God fill your mind so completely that nothing else can get in.

Never admit lack in any form. Strengthen your belief in omnipresence by keeping your containers filled to overflowing—your gasoline tank, the sugar bowl, the coal bin. Never tolerate that "run down at the heels" appearance or let your clothes get "out of press." Surround yourself with the essentials, even the small things, that give you a feeling of prosperity—plenty of food, dishes, towels, table linen; tooth paste, shaving cream and razor blades; shirts and clothes. Then remove from your home and office all that suggests lack, poverty, failure, inactivity.

Above all, never say "I cannot afford this or that." If God is omnipresent then you can afford anything and everything you need. Jesus said, "Ask and it shall be given unto you." Put yourself in a receiving attitude and you shall realize that all things are yours.

The Father, speaking to the prodigal's brother, said: "Son, thou art ever with me, and all that I have is thine." Do you believe that or are you still clinging to old beliefs, old clothes, old tires, old dresses or old shoes? Are you afraid to let the old things go for fear you will not get more? Haven't you learned that the real secret of prosperity is circulation; that the more you give the more you get. If "all things are yours," as Jesus said, and you believe it, why hang on to a fountain pen that won't work, your old billfold cluttered with useless receipts, cards and memoranda? Why look first for the price mark on merchandise? Why seek quantity instead of quality?

In general, why try to get along on a meager supply when god has given you "all things?"

Have you forgotten who you are that you contract life and shut yourself up in a small corner of God's Universe? "Enlarge the borders of your tent," and, as Jesus said, "Launch out into the deep." How can you expand your consciousness if you constantly are pinching your supply by seeking discounts and bargains—if you ask for abundance with your lips and limitation with your acts?

Why not look only for the best and buy only the best? Isn't it better even to get one thing at a time and have it good? Finally, how can you prove God's promises if you do not take Him at His word? How can you be rich if you live and act cheaply?

Jesus asked the father of the "possessed" child, "How long has he been like this?" And the father answer, "From a little child" . . . but if you possibly can, have compassion on us; and Jesus answered and said, "WHY DO YOU SAY POSSIBLY?"

All too long have we been brought up in the folds of ecclesiastical schools. Too often have we been "fed upon half truths," which, as Emerson said, "are the blackest lies." Our real Sonship has been distorted or suppressed. We have so long worshipped a God of wealth and poverty, of good and evil, heaven and hell, health and sickness, that good no longer seems possible as of Him or to us. Is it any wonder that Jesus expressed amazement at the father's words, "If you possibly can." Why do you say, "possibly"? "Is anything difficult for me?" "Is anything hard for me?"

How could you ask such a question? Are not all things possible with God? Why do you say possible? How long have you been in the far country living on husks? Shall we answer for you? Just as long as you have been worshipping God with only half your mind, half your heart, half your soul, half your strength, and half your faith.

And what is this little double mind that worships God and the devil, health and disease at the same time? And what are these impossible, incurable, insoluble, impregnable things which resist all your prayers and affirmation to and about the ONE and ONLY POWER? I'll tell you what they are. They are the frozen beliefs of a divided mind.

If "the law of the Lord is perfect," as the Psalmist said, then why do you say "possibly?" Isn't substance plastic and Spirit compelling; isn't it reasonable to expect that if a wrong relationship to the law has produced sickness and problems that a right relationship to the law will heal and solve them? Is it the Law that is at fault, or is your relationship to It?

The reason we are the victims of impoverished conditions and limited circumstances—the victims of all the things which keep us in a little, narrow sphere, is because we do not sense our real power as sons of God, because we never have learned how to assert our own Christhood and how to harness God's Power to our needs. We never have fully realized that God can do for us what we cannot do for ourselves.

We fumble about with little prayers and feeble demands, not sensing that we have within us (back of the personality and not of it) a power so great that if we would trust It and throw ourselves unhesitatingly upon It, It not only would heal supposed incurable disease but accomplish what seems to us impossible tasks. Integrated power is the most fabulous thing in the world and "has no limits except the limits of our own doubts."

In the New Testament, salvation from any difficulty whatever is predicated upon an entire and complete change of thought and a merging of the entire mind with God. That is what repentance means—a change of thinking and a new relationship to the law. It odes not mean giving up one kind of thought for another, "but forsaking one mode of thinking for another." It is a mental experience and until we recognize this fact there will be no progress in our work.

The basic thing in practice is not form, theory, system nor theology, but having the Mind of Christ, knowing Him in our own right. And how is this accomplished? By identifying our Christhood with His Christhood, by bringing our thinking up to the highest.

Jesus began with the assumption that man is God's son: that as God's son he not only is the rightful heir to all the riches of Heaven, but that he also is armed with a mighty power against any difficulty, disease or disaster that may threaten his life; that, when he comes into the consciousness of his Divine Sonship, all his needs will be met and all his desires fulfilled.

Jesus did not lay down any hard and fast rules for demonstrating truth, nor did He outline any particular system of thought. What he did teach, however, was that by keeping our thoughts raised to God, we would open ourselves to an influx of Divine Power which not only would keep us in a state of constant renewal, recreating and making us new creatures every day, but which also would meet our mental and Spiritual needs.

Jesus' whole plan of salvation was stated in six mighty words: "I and the Father are one." To Him, the union of the whole mentality and personality with God was the ultimate in spiritual endeavor and about which we were to accept no substitute. It is the guarantee not only of a triumphant, successful and harmonious life on earth, but of a continuing life after our work here is done.

UPLIFTED THOUGHT THE PRACTICAL APPROACH

We conclude, therefore, that uplifted thought (keeping God in the center of our consciousness and our mind on Him) is not only the most practical approach to God, but also the most dependable method for drawing His good into our lives. "My God shall supply all your needs according to His riches in glory by Jesus Christ." We hear much in religion today about our duty toward God, but the only duty we have toward God is "to see to it that Christ is really formed in us: that when we go into our consciousness, we come before the Presence of Christ."

Yes, dear reader, the ancient invitation of the church to "Lift up your hearts" sill is the open sesame to all spiritual achievement. When we have learned how to lift up our thoughts to God and keep them lifted up, then we shall no longer need to worry about specific ailments, claims and problems, for our needs will be met automatically. When our thoughts have been brought into harmony with Christ, then the Power will work for us according to our needs. When we have the Mind of Christ, then we shall do the things He did. He will continue His incarnation through us.

No more can we afford to think or act without Him, for we have found that as consciousness continues in God it gains in scope and power. Just as haphazard thinking (thought without God) demagnetizes the mind, lowers the resistance and attracts the wrong people and things, so uplifted (unified) thought magnetizes the mind, raises the resistance and attracts desirable conditions and people.

It makes no difference where you are or what your needs may be, if you return to the Father's House (lift up your thoughts to Him), all you have lost will return to you and that which you do not wish to retain will vanish. Is the will weak? Then it shall be strengthened. Is the body sick or diseased? Then it shall be made whole. Is money lacking? Then it shall be supplied. Is the problem insoluble? Then it shall be solved. Is there discord in your world? Then it shall be dissolved.

When you return home you return to your own, because the Father's House is the source of everything good that can possibly come into your life. To be at home is to be with God, and to be with God is to have every desire fulfilled.

Think of the glory of it all. Think of the happiness to come. When you touch Christ, you touch freedom and joy. When you touch Christ, you touch peace, wholeness and purity. When you touch Christ, you touch strength, health and truth.

When you touch Christ, you touch Heaven, dominion and power. When you touch Christ, you touch Life Eternal. When you touch Christ, you touch God. When you touch Christ, every right desire is realized and every dream made true. You touch everything that is desirable, perfect and true.

When you keep your thought lifted up to God, the past is all behind you and the future is all present. Divine Power flows into you, building you into a new creature and supplying all your needs. The Spirit of the Lord goes before you, making easy, successful and safe your way.

"If thou return to the Almighty, thou shalt be built up, thou shalt put away iniquity far from thy tabernacles.

"Thou shalt lay up gold as dust, and the gold of Ophir as the stones of the brooks.

"Yea, the Almighty shall be thy defence, and thou shalt have plenty of silver.

"For then shalt thou have thy delight in the Almighty, and shalt lift up thy face unto God.

"Thou shalt make thy prayer with him, and he shall hear thee, and thou shalt pay thy vows.

"Thou shalt also decree a thing, and it shall be established unto thee: and the light shall shine upon thy ways.

"When men are cast down, then thou shalt say, There is lifting up; and he shall save the humble person.

"He shall deliver the island of the innocent: and it is delivered by the pureness of thy hands."

Raisa - Mystic Alchemist

Energy Healing, Chakra Alignment, Sacred Geometry, Sound Healing

Tammy:
I was blessed with a healing session by Raisa last week. She felt like a friend and like-minded gentle soul with comforting Mother Mary essence pouring through her words. Raisa was so in-tuned to my blocks and traumas held within my field. She used her connection to ascended masters I've resonated with such as Yeshua, Mother Mary, Mary Magdalene, Lady Vesta & Amethyst and archangels Metatron, Michael and others to help clear these.

I was able to address childhood trauma situations to flip the stuck energy I've held onto over the years. She also picked up on a few traumatic past-life scenes that have affected my current life. I am an intuitive energy healer who truly felt the shift and healing within. I now feel so much lighter and have clarity regarding my path.

So much love and gratitude to you both, Raisa and Barry for presenting her to my world! (More Testimonials on following Pages)

Contact Raisa to book an Energy Healing
or Chakra Alignment session:
www.RaisinYourIsness.com
raisinyourisness@hotmail.com

Shannon:

This BEAUTIFUL sister...our Raisa... is a treasure beyond compare! After my experience in my personal session with Raisa... the ABSOLUTE confirmation I received, that could ONLY be confirmed by HER mind you... this session solidified EVERYTHING for me. I KNOW that this sister... she is a formidable, magnificent & IRREPLACEABLE component in this Earth plane story we all are invested in! IF YOU ARE DRAWN TO HER FOLLOW YOUR HEART

No other can do what SHE is gifted to do for YOU... YES YOU!

I LOVE YOU dear sister! I am forever grateful for what only you could do and DID for me! I would have happily paid any price for what you gave me! I URGE YOU ALL to schedule a session with this beloved one!

P.S. thank you Barry for sharing her with us all!

∞

Natasha:

I would like to thank Barry for introducing us to Raisa. I have had 2 consultations with her in the last month and I am in total awe of what transpired. Raisa is such a beautiful caring soul! She connected with me as though she has known me forever. Her love and dedication in assisting others is so touching. I had an amazing experience and some profound healing. I received a message from Jeshua which brought tears to my eyes. I could feel the LOVE in the message that was given to me and I will remember and cherish His message forever. Raisa has really helped me in confronting fears, trauma and past life karma. I have found the reason for my skin problems which I never would have thought it'd be possible. It is amazing what guilt and shame from past lives can actually do to your body. Her healing and that from our Angelic beings has really made a huge difference in my life. I can feel it in my energy. Raisa has a lovely sense of humour, always reminding you not to take life and yourself so seriously. I really feel like a heavy weight has been lifted off my soul. Thank you so much! Much Love!

∞

Ariel:

Raisa... Divine Raisa... You are a Treasure to this Life, and I thank All That Is, and this also Treasured YT channel for the priceless blessing which was our session this AM. Every moment of the session was a fractal explosion of wonderful intuitive & divinely guided perfection. I honor your sincere, caring, graceful, playful, soothing, encouraging, transformational, empowering, and so beautiful demonstration / embodiment of Goddess energy and presence. I am so honored & thankful to have been guided to You. To have invested in the patience, time, energy, and resources to share sacred healing and uplifting time with You. I will remember the session Always. And I will look forward to any and all ways our Creator deems it harmonious to connect again. I could go on and on and on, so please accept my parting acknowledgment of your blessing to this realm, my Heart & Spirt, my Life, and the Lives of all those who may be positively impacted via your assistance. Blessings, and Gratitude, a thousand times over and over again. Namaste... Namaste... Namaste...

∞

B.G.

I have just finished a healing session with Raisa. The experience was remarkable! I am still buzzing! I heard about her from this channel, so thank you deeply Barry!

Raisa is so lovely to talk to, and intuitively guided, knows how to get to the hidden roots of our issues. She calls upon ascended masters, archangels and such to do deep energetic clearing and healing work. It was like being guided through the deep layers of myself, releasing the things that don't serve me and filling every cell with light. I purged, and I absorbed new energy, and came out feeling uplifted and renewed. Raisa helped me to find things in myself that I had been cut off from, and to heal wounds I had tried to bury. She has also given me helpful ideas to continue to improve things my life.

I am so blessed to have found Raisa, and ever grateful for the healing work she has done. She is as authentic as they come. Truly an earth angel! Thank you, thank you, thank you!

YouTube

YouTube Channels of Interest:

Giving Voice to the Wisdom of the Ages

Over 5,000 audios, hundreds of
Spiritual and Metaphysical
audio books including
Robert A Russell, Dr Murdo MacDonald Bayne,
Napoleon Hill, Jeshua, Kryon and many more.

I AM Meditations and Affirmations

Hundreds of I AM Meditations,
Daily affirmations and more.

Raisin' Your Isness

Metaphysical Musings, Channelings,
Sound Healing Songs

.

www.ingramcontent.com/pod-product-compliance
Lightning Source LLC
Chambersburg PA
CBHW021342090426
42742CB00008B/703